Glorious Victory

WITNESS TO HISTORY

Peter Charles Hoffer and Williamjames Hull Hoffer, *Series Editors*

William Thomas Allison, *My Lai: An American Atrocity in the Vietnam War*

Peter Charles Hoffer, *When Benjamin Franklin Met the Reverend Whitefield: Enlightenment, Revival, and the Power of the Printed Word*

Williamjames Hull Hoffer, *The Caning of Charles Sumner: Honor, Idealism, and the Origins of the Civil War*

Tim Lehman, *Bloodshed at Little Bighorn: Sitting Bull, Custer, and the Destinies of Nations*

Daniel R. Mandell, *King Philip's War: Colonial Expansion, Native Resistance, and the End of Indian Sovereignty*

Erik R. Seeman, *The Huron-Wendat Feast of the Dead: Indian-European Encounters in Early North America*

Peter Charles Hoffer, *Prelude to Revolution: The Salem Gunpower Raid of 1775*

Michael Dennis, *Blood on Steel: Chicago Steelworkers and the Strike of 1937*

Benjamin F. Alexander, *Coxey's Army: Popular Protest in the Gilded Age*

John R. Van Atta, *Wolf by the Ears: The Missouri Crisis, 1819–1821*

Glorious Victory

Andrew Jackson and the Battle of New Orleans

DONALD R. HICKEY

Johns Hopkins University Press | *Baltimore*

© 2015 Johns Hopkins University Press
All rights reserved. Published 2015
Printed in the United States of America on acid-free paper

9 8 7 6 5 4 3 2 1

Johns Hopkins University Press
2715 North Charles Street
Baltimore, Maryland 21218-4363
www.press.jhu.edu

Cataloging-in-Publication data on file at the Library of Congress

ISBN 978-1-4214-1703-5 (hardcover; alk. paper)
ISBN 978-1-4214-1704-2 (paperback; alk. paper)
ISBN 978-1-4214-1705-9 (electronic)

A catalog record for this book is available from the British Library.

Special discounts are available for bulk purchases of this book.
For more information, please contact Special Sales at 410-516-6936 or
specialsales@press.jhu.edu.

Johns Hopkins University Press uses environmentally friendly book
materials, including recycled text paper that is composed of at least
30 percent post-consumer waste, whenever possible.

For my siblings: Linda, Jim, and Dave

Glorious Victory!

FROM NEW-ORLEANS

The Enemy, attacking our entrenched Army on the 8th, [was] beaten and repulsed by Jackson and his brave associates, with great slaughter.

Washington *National Intelligencer* extra, February 4, 1815

Contents

Preface

MOST SCHOLARS know that writing a book can put them on an emotional roller coaster. You start with what seems like a great idea, but before long what began as an exciting project turns into a burdensome chore. You have to do far more work than you anticipated, and you may encounter problems so intractable that you consider abandoning the project altogether. If you do finish, you can't wait to get the manuscript off your desk and out of your life. And yet you have to wait a year before your book is in print, and in the meantime there is more drudgery: reading the proofs and preparing the index. Such is the relief when your work is truly done that you may greet the actual publication of the book with a shrug. In sum, however much you might like to have a book to your credit, writing one is rarely easy. This is aptly illustrated by the time-honored saying that everyone wants to have written a book but nobody wants to write one.

Happily, my experience with this book has been different. Except for a small setback near the end, it has been a joy to work on throughout. It helps that it is a short book on a subject that I consider both interesting and important. I ran into no major obstacles along the way, a reflection, no doubt, of the fine spade work done by those who came before me. The three principal topics of this book—the War of 1812, Andrew Jackson, and the Battle of New Orleans—have all received a fair amount of scholarly attention, which made my job a lot easier.

I am indebted to Bob Brugger at Johns Hopkins University Press for suggesting that I write this volume for the Witness to History series. Along with Dan Feller, Bob also helped me frame my story. Series editor Peter Hoffer, Charles Berthold, and Mark Cheathem made a number of helpful suggestions for improving the work. I also profited from a close reading of the final draft by John Quist and by my always careful and efficient copyeditor, Kathryn Roberts Morrow, and I benefited from the patience and attention to detail shown by Mary Lou Kenney, a senior production editor at Johns Hopkins University Press.

I am indebted to Jason Wiese of the Historic New Orleans Collection for supplying information on Andrew Jackson and the weather on the day of the main battle and to Bobby Ticknor at the same institution for expediting my request to use a pair of illustrations. Bill Cook provided information on the "coffin handbills" in the election of 1828, and Peter Broadbent helped me get the number of future presidents who benefited from the War of 1812 right. Two colleagues at Wayne State College, geographer Randy Bertolas and librarian Charissa Loftis, helped me track down other information that I sought.

I owe a special debt to Terri Headley at the Interlibrary Loan Desk for securing just about everything that I asked for and for doing so in a timely fashion. Bob Cronan of Lucidity Information Design created the maps. Finally, I want to thank my wife, Connie Clark, who carefully read the entire manuscript several times and not only caught a host of errors but also made a number of valuable recommendations for improving the work. Connie also did the bulk of the work in preparing the index.

As always in military history, the numbers—of those engaged in a battle and of casualties—are sometimes difficult to nail down. I used what I thought were the most credible numbers, and I frequently rounded them. Also, in the interest of making this work more readable, I modernized the spelling and punctuation in contemporary quotations but left most of the capitalization intact because I think it was often used for emphasis.

Glorious Victory

prologue

America at a Crossroads

SHORTLY BEFORE sunrise on January 8, 1815, Major General Edward Pakenham ordered a Congreve rocket fired into the air. This was the signal for the first wave of some 5,300 British troops south of New Orleans to attack the main American line 650 yards to the north. Pakenham, a 37-year-old battle-tested officer, was the brother-in-law of the Duke of Wellington, the preeminent British military figure of the age. One of his subordinates described him as "a hero, a soldier, a man of ability in every sense of the word."[1] Pakenham had the support of a tested officer corps, and most of the troops he commanded at New Orleans had seen fighting in Europe or America.

The American line, which extended a mile from the Mississippi River on the west to a cypress swamp on the east, was formidable, an earthwork that was as much as 20 feet thick and 8 feet high. It was manned by some 4,700 troops under the command of Major General Andrew Jackson, an able and experienced officer. Although many of the men had taken part in Jackson's previous campaigns against the Creek Indians, his army did not look very impressive, consisting of some U.S. Army and Navy units but mostly militia and volunteers from Louisiana, Tennessee, Kentucky, and Mississippi; two black units (including one unit of refugees from Haiti); a band of Choctaw

Indians; and some seamen belonging to a group of lawless raiders known as the Baratarian pirates.

The British had launched the campaign for New Orleans six weeks earlier, when a large armada had departed Jamaica for the Gulf Coast. The Redcoats appeared just 8 miles south of their objective on December 23, before anyone knew they were near. Getting there had not been easy, and their suffering only got worse. Rain dogged the troops from the moment they reached Louisiana, making it difficult to stay dry, and at night the temperatures plunged so low that some soldiers froze to death. No one recorded the temperature on the day of the battle, but it was probably around 40 degrees. Fog covered the battlefield. By late morning the bone-chilling mist gave way to a steady rain that continued throughout the day.

Cold and wet, the British were unable to build fires or protective shelters because when they did they drew artillery fire from American batteries. Everyone and everything was covered with mud, and no one could take a step without sinking into the mire. Four decades later a naval officer who was only 19 in 1815 recalled his experience: "I remember to this day," he said, "how wretchedly off I was about the shoes, which stuck in the mud every now and then, and I was so tired I felt half inclined to leave my heavy great coat in the mud, but we stuck together and went on. . . . I slept in the mud the remainder of the night, and daylight found me a horrid mess."[2]

The only food available was naval rations—mostly salted meat, ship's biscuit, and grog (that is, watered-down rum)—and keeping mud off even this meager fare was no easy task. Disease took a growing toll on the British, especially dysentery, which caused extreme diarrhea, but even in winter plenty of other diseases stalked armies in the field. There were also losses from sniper fire. Tennessee and Choctaw sharpshooters took special pleasure in slipping out at night into the no-man's-land that separated the two armies and targeting British pickets and other soldiers who had wandered away from camp. Adding to the British frustration was the lack of any success against Jackson. As members of a successful British army that had been victorious over Napoleon's finest in Europe, the invaders referred to Jackson's motley group of amateurs as "Dirty Shirts." Yet in three preliminary engagements south of New Orleans, the "Dirty Shirts" had prevailed. The coming battle thus offered the British a chance for redemption as well as the prospect of escaping the cold, rain, mud, and hunger.

Jackson's men had to contend with some of the same problems as the British, but they enjoyed a greater measure of material comfort. The U.S. Army ration—beef or pork, bread, and whiskey—was modest and monotonous, but everyone got his fair share. Plus, anyone could buy additional food from vendors who visited from New Orleans. Warehouses there were so jam-packed with grain and other foodstuffs that prices remained low. The residents of New Orleans also were generous in sharing what they had with the men charged with defending the city. Besides being well fed, the American troops could also get out of the weather by building fires and taking refuge in tents or makeshift shelters behind the formidable American line.

For most American soldiers the entire campaign must have seemed like an exotic adventure. Unlike the British, who were professionals accustomed to campaigning abroad, the Americans were mostly militia and volunteers, many not much more than 20 years old, who had probably never been this far from home. As the largest city in the West, New Orleans was almost surely the most impressive city they had ever seen, and with its decidedly French and Catholic character it bore little resemblance to other cities and towns in the nation. Simply conversing with local residents posed a challenge because most spoke only French. As a wide-open city with gambling, prostitution, and no restrictions on the Sabbath, it must have seemed to most American troops as if they had left the United States.

Jackson always kept his men on a tight leash. To prevent anyone from leaving to sample the delights of the Crescent City, he posted sentinels 400 yards to the rear of his line. But his troops were accustomed to his commitment to duty and discipline, and this had little negative effect on the mood of the army. In sharp contrast to the British, the morale of the U.S. troops remained high. Their confidence in Jackson was unbounded. Those who had served with him in the Creek War knew what he was like. Those who had not, knew him by reputation.

Although "Old Hickory" (as Jackson was called) was a product of the hardscrabble Carolina backcountry, after moving to Tennessee he had made a successful career as a lawyer, merchant, and land speculator, joining the local landholding and slave-owning aristocracy. He might have spent his life as a typical member of Tennessee's gentry had he not become a major general in the militia, parlaying an intuitive grasp of military measures and an iron will into victory after victory over the Creeks. He was rewarded with a commission

Jackson rallying his troops at New Orleans (detail). (The Granger Collection, New York)

as major general in the regular army and command over the Southwest and Gulf Coast.

During the entire campaign at New Orleans, Jackson was constantly busy, overseeing everything that he could and assigning what he could not do to trusted subordinates. His attention to detail was one of the keys to his success, and he often sacrificed food and sleep to attend to his duties. He kept abreast of enemy troop movements with an extensive intelligence system, and except for the unexpected appearance of the British south of New Orleans, there were no surprises. The British had already taken Jackson's measure, first by sparring with him on the Gulf Coast and then in the preliminary battles near New Orleans. They had developed a grudging respect for the U.S. commander, but they might be pardoned for thinking they could scatter his ragtag army, just as they had done to many other American forces in the War of 1812.

If the British prevailed in the coming battle, the road to New Orleans would be open. They would control not only the city but the entire lower Mississippi River basin. Reports later surfaced that the British planned to sack the city if they won. And since Pakenham was expected to establish a government in any territory he conquered, one might well wonder whether that territory would ever be restored to the United States. The coming battle might thus determine the fate of New Orleans and the Southwest and fundamentally alter the course of American history.

With Pakenham's signal rocket illuminating the dark sky, the British troops began to trudge through the mist, mud, and muck toward Jackson's line. The Battle of New Orleans was about to begin. The one-sided carnage that followed in the next 30 minutes would change America and stun the world.

1 Completing the Revolution

THE UNITED STATES found itself at a crossroads at New Orleans because the War of 1812 had not gone as expected. No one on either side of the Atlantic really wanted this war. In Great Britain, all eyes were on a much more important conflict that was under way with France, and British leaders saw an American war as an unwelcome distraction. But they preferred war with America to giving up maritime policies that might produce defeat in Europe. Britain's subjects in Canada also had no desire to wage war against their neighbors to the south, but they were determined to protect their homeland and preserve their ties with the mother country. Indians, most of whom sided with the British, also wanted to be left alone, but they, too, were willing to fight to defend their lands and preserve their way of life.

Even the United States, which initiated the war, was a reluctant belligerent. Americans wanted nothing more than to remain at peace so they could continue to turn a profit in a war-torn world, but they were willing to go to war to defend their rights on the high seas. They believed that Britain's maritime practices threatened U.S. sovereignty and that war was necessary to vindicate their independence. War was needed, in other words, to complete the

American Revolution by showing the world that no nation, least of all their former oppressors, could trample on U.S. rights with impunity.

The Road to War

The War of 1812 was a by-product of the French Revolutionary and Napoleonic Wars (1793–1815). This was the final phase of a longer period of Anglo-French conflict, sometimes called the Second Hundred Years War (1689–1815). The two European powers were fighting to determine which would dominate Europe and the wider world. In the pursuit of victory the European powers and their allies repeatedly violated American rights.

The central question that American policy makers wrestled with throughout the period from 1793 to 1812 was this: How could a second-rate power like the United States protect its rights and promote its interests in a world at war? For Federalists, who controlled the government in the 1790s, and for Democratic-Republicans, who controlled it after 1801, this was the million-dollar question, and it had no easy answer.

European encroachments on American rights increased after 1805, when two decisive battles left Britain, already the dominant sea power, and France, unmistakably the dominant land power, even more formidable. At sea, in the Battle of Trafalgar on October 21, Britain smashed a Franco-Spanish fleet. Six weeks later, on December 2, Napoleon, the emperor of France, defeated a large Russo-Austrian army in the Battle of Austerlitz. Thereafter, the contest between these two powerful foes resembled a battle between a shark and a tiger. Unable to get at one another directly, Britain and France targeted neutral trade, and the United States was caught in the middle.

The two leading causes of the War of 1812 were the British Orders-in-Council and the British practice of impressment. The Orders-in-Council (1807–09) sharply curtailed U.S. trade with the European continent. Under the authority of these decrees, the British between 1807 and 1812 seized and condemned some 400 American merchant ships. This represented a huge property loss for the United States and drove some merchants out of business.

No less galling was the British practice of impressment to secure seamen (then called "tars" because they were often covered with the tar they used to seal their ships and preserve their rigging). From 1793 to 1812, the manpower needs of the British navy soared from 36,000 to 114,000, which left most

British warships shorthanded. To fill out its crews, the Royal Navy claimed the right to stop American merchant vessels on the high seas and to impress (that is, conscript) British tars, who constituted between one-sixth and one-third of the American crews. Not only did this practice sometimes leave American ships dangerously shorthanded, but many American citizens—perhaps 6,000 to 9,000 between 1803 and 1812—got caught in the British dragnet.

There was little that the U.S. government could do to protect its citizens from this practice. It issued crude passports, known as "protections," to try to safeguard Americans from impressment, but these documents contained only a brief physical description of the seamen to whom they were issued. It was not difficult for British tars to acquire the documents by theft, purchase, or fraud. For a dollar, it was said, any British seaman in an American port could become an American citizen. Under these circumstances, it is hardly surprising that the Royal Navy refused to honor the documents.

The Democratic-Republican administration in Washington was unwilling to spend money on defense measures to protect American rights. Instead it resorted to economic sanctions. Between 1806 and 1811 Congress adopted a series of trade restrictions designed to force Britain (and, to a lesser degree, France) to cease their violations of American rights. The "restrictive system," as these measures were collectively called, won no concessions from the European belligerents but instead boomeranged on the United States, undermining prosperity and cutting into government revenue. The worst of the trade restrictions was President Thomas Jefferson's painful Embargo, which prohibited American ships and goods from leaving port for 15 months, from December 1807 to March 1809.

By the end of 1811, many Democratic-Republican leaders had concluded that without British concessions the young republic's only option was war. President James Madison agreed. The 61-year old veteran U.S. statesman summoned Congress to an early meeting in 1811. In his opening address on November 5, he recommended war preparations and found a willing audience among a group of young House members known as "War Hawks." Too young to remember the horrors of the American Revolution, the War Hawks were willing to risk another British war to vindicate the nation's rights and independence. Headed by 34-year-old Henry Clay of Kentucky, a first-term congressman who turned the largely ceremonial post of speaker into a position of power, the War Hawks pushed through a series of war preparations between December 1811 and April 1812.

American officials then marked time to see if the threat of war won any concessions from the British. When none were forthcoming, the president on June 1 sent a secret message to Congress recommending a declaration of war. Congress took up a war bill in secret session and adopted it by a vote of 79–49 in the House and 19–13 in the Senate. Madison signed the bill into law on June 18, and with his signature the War of 1812 began.

A Risky Decision

On the surface, the U.S. decision to go to war in 1812 was risky, if not foolhardy. The war preparations were far from complete, and the nation was ill-equipped to launch any combat operations. The U.S. Army, about 12,000 strong when the war began, consisted mostly of raw recruits. Senior officers were political appointees or relics from the Revolution who had lost their taste for battle. According to Winfield Scott, one of the rising stars in the army who would distinguish himself in both the War of 1812 and the Mexican War, "the old officers had, very generally, sunk into either sloth, ignorance, or habits of intemperate drinking." Even a year into the war, Peter B. Porter, a congressional War Hawk and senior officer in the New York militia, reported that "Our Army is full of men, fresh from Lawyer shops & counting rooms, who know little of the physical force of man—of the proper means of sustaining & improving it—or even the mode of its application."[1]

The War Department was understaffed and lacked the administrative machinery to sustain the war effort. According to War Hawk George M. Troup of Georgia, "In the wretched, deplorably wretched organization of the War Department, it was impossible either to begin the war or to conduct it."[2] The nation had few good roads—even fewer in the West—and thus had to depend on available waterways to move men and material around. As a result, supplying the war effort efficiently, particularly on distant fronts, was never easy and at times impossible.

The Navy Department was more efficient. The U.S. Navy had well-constructed warships, good officers, and experienced crews. But with only 17 ships, the Navy was unlikely to be much of a presence on the oceans of the world. The gap would have to be filled by privateers—privately armed ships fitted out to cruise against the enemy's commerce—but they could provide no protection to the nation's coast or commerce.

The task of waging war was further complicated by domestic opposition. Every Federalist in Congress voted against the declaration of war. So, too, did nearly 20 percent of the Democratic-Republicans. Although most Democratic-Republicans fell into line once the decision was made, Federalists did not. They refused to support bills to raise men and money, to promote privateering, or to restrict trade with the enemy. They also discouraged enlistments in the army and subscriptions to the war loans. The only warlike measures they were willing to support were those for expanding the navy or building coastal fortifications, which they considered a good long-term investment in the nation's future.

The nation's enemy in the war was formidable. Great Britain was one of the two most powerful nations in the world. With over 500 warships, she had long dominated the oceans and with good reason was known as "Mistress of the Seas." The British also had a veteran army nearly 250,000 strong. Only 10,000 of those troops were stationed in Canada, the only likely theater of land operations, but the officers were battle-tested and the men, even those without combat experience, were nonetheless reliable and disciplined regulars. Moreover, the British could count on their native allies, who were superb scouts, trackers, and skirmishers. The Indians also had a reputation for ferocity and a penchant for torturing prisoners. Their presence on a battlefield could tip the balance by panicking even a veteran force.

Most Democratic-Republicans understood that the nation was ill-prepared for war but were willing to take the risk anyway. In the colorful language of Congressman Robert Wright of Maryland, they were willing "to get married, & buy the furniture afterwards."[3] How, then, did they expect to win? For one thing, there was some hope that no fighting would actually be necessary. Many Democratic-Republican leaders were convinced that the British were simply unaware of how angry Americans were over the violations of their rights.

Secretary of State James Monroe thought that the administration had relied too long on trade restrictions and had talked too much about war without doing anything. As a result, "the British Government has not believed us" and thus "the argument of War, with its consequences, has not had its due weight with that Government."[4] Charles Cutts, a Democratic-Republican senator from New Hampshire, made a similar point. "I have long since adopted the opinion," he said, "that if Great Britain would be once convinced that war with this country would be inevitable unless she receded from her unjust pretensions all causes of irritation would be speedily removed."[5] If these Democratic-Republicans were right, then the declaration of war alone might be enough of a shock to win British concessions on the maritime issues in dispute.

What if the British did not agree to American demands? There was no way the United States could challenge Britain at sea, but it could menace Britain's North American provinces, which then were collectively referred to as Canada. The United States had a huge population advantage over Canada—7.7 million to 500,000—and the allegiance of many people living in Canada was suspect. Although the old Loyalist population that had migrated to Canada after the American Revolution was fiercely loyal to the mother country, the same could not be said for the original French population, which accounted for two-thirds of the people in Lower Canada (now the province of Quebec). No less problematic was the loyalty of the many Americans who after 1792 had migrated to Upper Canada (present-day Ontario) to take advantage of free land and low taxes. By 1812 they accounted for about 60 percent of the population of Upper Canada. Although British officials optimistically referred to these immigrants as the "Late Loyalists," most would probably be neutral, if not pro-American, in any war with the United States. Of the half million people living in Canada, the British could probably count on the loyalty of no more than 150,000.

Most Democratic-Republicans assumed that American troops would be welcomed in Canada as liberators. The governor of New York predicted that "one-half of the Militia of [Canada] would join our standard."[6] Any fighting that was necessary was unlikely to be prolonged or extensive. Henry Clay thought that "the militia of Kentucky are alone competent to place Montreal and Upper Canada at our feet." Thomas Jefferson concurred. Now in retirement but following matters from Monticello, he claimed that seizing all of Canada west of Quebec would be "a mere matter of marching" and that the rest of Canada would fall the following year.[7] John Randolph of Roanoke, a Democratic-Republican critic of the war, was incredulous of this view. He mocked those who expected what he derisively called "a holiday campaign." With "no expense of blood or treasure on our part," he said, "Canada is to conquer herself—she is to be subdued by the principles of fraternity."[8]

Republicans also counted on Britain's inability to offer much help to Canada. After all, Britain's top priority was winning her war against France.

Her army was tied up fighting the French in Spain and protecting other British possessions in the far corners of the world. Her mighty fleet was already spread thin, defending the homeland from a possible French invasion and carrying out other duties around the globe. The Napoleonic Wars had been raging for a decade, and with no end in sight, Democratic-Republicans had every reason to believe that Canada would get little help from Great Britain. Moreover, with war threatening between France and Russia, Britain's position on the Continent might become even more desperate. Although Americans could not know it, five days after the U.S. declaration of war, Napoleon launched a huge invasion of Russia with some 600,000 men. If, as seemed likely, Napoleon defeated Russia, his position on the Continent would be even stronger, perhaps unassailable.

Of course, none of this played out as Democratic-Republicans expected. Great Britain did not cave in to American demands. Napoleon was defeated in Russia, which marked the beginning of a shift in his fortunes in the European war. Moreover the British and their native allies in Canada proved a much tougher foe than anyone in America anticipated. The U.S. Army was not up to the task of conquering Canada, and neither short-term volunteers nor militia were of much help. Beyond this, the logistical challenges of waging war in the North American wilderness proved nearly insurmountable. Within two years, instead of conquering Canada, the United States found itself on the defensive and in the throes of a national crisis that threatened to destroy the nation.

Tecumseh and Tippecanoe

Complicating the U.S. decision to go to war in 1812 was an Indian war that had erupted in the Old Northwest the previous fall. William Henry Harrison, who served as both the governor of the Indiana Territory and U.S. Indian agent, had imposed a series of increasingly dubious land cession treaties on the native population between 1803 and 1809. Harrison relied heavily on compliant Indians who had been plied with liquor and presents and who often had little claim to the lands they were surrendering. The climax came in 1809, when the Treaty of Fort Wayne transferred 3 million acres to the United States.

This was the last straw for many natives in the region, who became more militant and openly sought a British alliance. Heading this group were two

Shawnee brothers: Tenskwatawa (better known as the Prophet), who had launched a native spiritual revival in 1805, and Tecumseh, a gifted leader who transformed the religious movement into a political and military alliance. The two brothers established a camp called Prophetstown near the confluence of the Wabash and Tippecanoe rivers in Indiana Territory. At the same time, the more militant natives stepped up their raids on U.S. settlements.

To end the raids and break up Prophetstown, Harrison, who knew that Tecumseh was away on a recruiting mission in the South, marched a mixed force of 1,000 regulars and volunteer militia to the Indian encampment. In the early morning hours of November 7, 1811, he was attacked by some 500 natives. Although Harrison broke the native attack and then burned Prophetstown, his force suffered heavy casualties. The victory was far less one-sided and decisive than he reported. The Battle of Tippecanoe touched off the Northwest Indian War of 1811, which blended into the War of 1812 seven months later when the United States declared war on Britain.

Strategy and Supply

The U.S. government had no war planning agency in 1812. In the run-up to the war neither the president nor anyone in the War Department gave much thought to strategy. No one apparently wondered how the British had taken Quebec in 1759. There was no appreciation of the favorable combination of circumstances that had made that campaign a success: A large and well-drilled British army had made the assault; the Royal Navy had offered indispensable support from the St. Lawrence River; and the French, needing to protect their supply lines to the interior, had met the British on the Plains of Abraham because their defenses on this western side of Quebec were weak. None of these conditions existed for the United States in 1812.

Not only did U.S. leaders ignore the British campaign of 1759, but they also failed to learn the lessons of the American campaign against Canada in 1775–76, when Montreal was taken but an assault on Quebec had been a costly failure. Instead, officials in Washington assumed that victory would be assured by the nation's population advantage combined with the welcome they expected to receive in Canada.

On the eve of war American strategy was devised by Major General Henry Dearborn, a 61-year-old veteran of the Revolution who had served as

Jefferson's secretary of war and was given the senior command on the northern border. Dearborn recommended a three-pronged assault on Canada, with one army advancing across the Detroit River at the western end of Lake Erie, a second army invading across the Niagara River at the eastern end of the lake, and a third army heading north from Plattsburgh along a traditional invasion route that followed Lake Champlain and the Richelieu River. This strategy would appease Madison's western constituents, taking advantage of western enthusiasm for the war, and offer a chance to win the Indian war that had erupted in the region the previous fall. But it would also commit too many American resources too far west to secure the conquest of Canada.

British strategy, devised by Sir George Prevost, the 45-year-old governor-general of Canada, was defensive. Prevost planned to rely heavily on the regulars who were in Canada when war broke out and on native allies, most notably the western Indians led by Tecumseh and the Prophet and the Grand River Iroquois under the leadership of the mixed-blood Mohawk chief, John Norton. Prevost also planned to rely on militia for both combat and support duties.

Prevost made the defense of Quebec his top priority. Although the Royal Navy could ferry supplies and a few reinforcements across the Atlantic, the governor could not count on much aid from the mother country as long as the war in Europe continued. He was willing to abandon Upper Canada if needed, but that need never arose. The Royal Navy could protect Quebec about six months of the year, and by establishing a naval blockade and mounting raids along the U.S. coast, it could also cut off American trade, deprive the federal government of revenue, and bring the war home to Americans who lived on the seaboard.

British supply lines to Canada ran 3,000 miles across the Atlantic, and in the Age of Sail the typical voyage took six to eight weeks. It was another 1,200 miles from the Gulf of St. Lawrence via the St. Lawrence River and the Great Lakes to Fort Amherstburg on the Detroit River. The main British supply line across Canada was not only long but exposed. The St. Lawrence River lay along the border with the United States and thus at times was an active theater of military operations. It is not clear why the United States did not do more to cut this vital link in Britain's supply route.

American supply routes were shorter and less exposed, running perpendicular to the border. But without good roads or convenient waterways, supplying troops that were campaigning in the north was no easy task. From the beginning, the U.S. supply service was undermined by a chronic shortage of money, unreliable private contractors, and a lack of necessary administrative machinery to provide oversight.

The troops paid the price for this lack of support. Pay was usually in arrears, food was often inedible or in short supply, and clothing and other vital supplies sometimes reached the men too late to prevent suffering. The troops were so badly provided for, concluded one general near the end of the war, that the number killed in battle was "trifling" compared to losses from other causes, mostly disease.[9]

Given the problems of supplying troops on the frontier, control of the waterways was crucial. Whoever controlled the lakes and rivers controlled the surrounding territory. But control of the waterways did not guarantee success, especially for offensive operations. An entrenched army charged with defending a position always had a significant advantage because it did not have to move, and it could stockpile whatever food, war material, or other supplies that might be needed to hold its position. This explains why offensive operations so often failed and why, on the battlefield at least, the war ended in a draw.

The War in the North

1812: America Invades Canada

The three-pronged invasion launched by the United States in 1812 was slow to develop and ended in disaster. In the West, Brigadier General William Hull, a 59-year-old veteran of the Revolution who had recently suffered a stroke, was in charge. His men had so little confidence in him that behind his back they called him "the Old Lady." On the eve of war, Hull began the laborious task of cutting a road through the Black Swamp (wetlands that have since been drained) in northern Ohio in order to link Urbana to Detroit, nearly 200 miles away. By the time Hull reached Detroit on July 5 with a mixed force of some 2,000 regulars and militia, his baggage and correspondence had fallen into British hands. The size and disposition of his army were known to the enemy.

Hull learned that Fort Mackinac, located on an island nearly 300 miles to the north in Lake Michigan, had fallen to an Anglo-Indian force on July 17. Fearing that he would be overrun by Indians pouring in from the north, he took refuge with his army in Fort Detroit. Shortly thereafter, an Anglo-Indian force led by 43-year-old Major General Isaac Brock and Tecumseh laid siege to the American fort, demanding Hull's surrender. On August 16, unable to maintain his supply lines to Ohio and fearing a native massacre if he resisted, Hull complied with the demand. The day before, a small American force that had abandoned Fort Dearborn in Chicago did not get very far before being attacked by a large band of Indians who killed a number of the soldiers and civilians after surrender terms had been agreed to. This was remembered as the Fort Dearborn Massacre.

Hull's surrender exposed American settlements in the region to native raids and led to pleas for government protection. Because he had defeated the Indians at Tippecanoe in 1811, 39-year-old William Henry Harrison had the confidence of the West and was chosen as Hull's replacement. Harrison built his army and stockpiled supplies, but bad weather forced him to postpone any major campaign until the following spring. Instead, he sent a large advance party under Brigadier General James Winchester to prepare winter quarters on the Maumee River near present-day Toledo, Ohio.

Following his own counsels, Winchester decided to march to Frenchtown (now Monroe, Michigan) on the River Raisin to protect local inhabitants. A British and Indian force under Colonel Henry Procter defeated Winchester and captured his army on January 22, 1813. The following day, Indians mas-

sacred at least 30 of the wounded American prisoners who had been left behind when Procter withdrew to Upper Canada. "The savages *were suffered to
commit every depredation upon our wounded,*" reported a group of American
officers; "*many were tomahawked, and many were burned alive in the houses.*"[10]
Winchester's campaign gave westerners a battle cry—"Remember the Raisin"
—but little else.

The war at the other end of Lake Erie across the Niagara River did not go
any better for the United States. In charge of this campaign was 47-year-old
Major General Stephen Van Rensselaer of the New York militia, a prominent
and influential landowner known as "the last of the patroons" (aristocratic
Dutch landholders). Van Rensselaer had no military experience and relied
heavily for advice on his younger kinsman, 38-year-old Lieutenant Colonel
Solomon Van Rensselaer, who had fought in the Indian wars of the 1790s.
Even so, the senior Van Rensselaer managed the campaign badly. As a result,
another army was lost.

In the early morning hours of October 13, the younger Van Rensselaer led
an advance party that consisted mostly of regulars across the Niagara River,
landing 6 miles south of Fort George. Meeting stiff resistance, Van Rensselaer was wounded four times and his men were pinned down on the shoreline until a path was found to Queenston Heights above. The Americans took
possession of the heights. General Brock, who had returned from Detroit to
take charge on the Niagara, was killed in a British counterattack. The American force, now under the command of Lieutenant Colonel Winfield Scott,
had grown to about 1,000 men. Pinned down by a party of Grand River Iroquois led by John Norton, the Americans badly needed reinforcements to
hold their position on the heights.

New York militia on the American side were ordered to cross the river but
refused. Spooked by the native war whoops coming from the other side and
by the dead and wounded who were being ferried back to the American side,
the citizen soldiers claimed they could not be ordered to serve outside of
American territory. Without reinforcements, Scott's force on the heights was
overwhelmed by a British counterattack led by Brock's replacement, Major
General Roger Sheaffe. Scott had little choice but to surrender. In all, 1,300
Americans were killed or captured in the Battle of Queenston Heights.

Nor did the United States enjoy any greater success farther east. An
American army was supposed to follow Lake Champlain and the Richelieu
River into Canada for an assault on Montreal. Since Montreal and Quebec

anchored British defenses along the St. Lawrence, this operation should have taken priority over others in 1812. But Henry Dearborn, who was in charge of this theater of operations, had no interest in campaigning and frittered his time away recruiting troops and planning fortifications far from the Canadian border. Nicknamed "Granny" by his troops, Dearborn sought to leave the campaigning to a subordinate. When that man became ill, Dearborn himself had to take the field. By then it was November, too late in the season to begin an operation so far north.

Dearborn halted when he reached the Canadian border. Colonel Zebulon Pike, the 33-year-old famed army explorer, was with Dearborn and secured permission to lead 500 men into Canada to attack an Indian camp that was thought to be nearby. Failing to find the camp, Pike clashed with a British force at Lacolle Mill. In the confused nighttime fighting, Pike took some casualties from friendly fire and then withdrew to the United States. By now Dearborn realized that his 2,500 militia were unwilling to march into Canada, and although he still had 3,500 regulars under his command, he used the refusal of the militia as an excuse to call off the campaign and go into winter quarters at Plattsburgh, New York. A Democratic-Republican critic described the campaign as a "miscarriage, without even [the] heroism of disaster."[11]

The entire U.S. campaign of 1812 was a failure. The United States had lost three armies (at Detroit, Frenchtown, and Queenston Heights) and had surrendered three key forts in the West (at Mackinac, Detroit, and Chicago). The British now occupied Michigan Territory, and their native allies raided the exposed U.S. settlements at will. The United States could claim no victories and found itself further from the conquest of Canada than when the war began.

The failure was the result of an undersized and raw army being led by incompetent senior officers and poorly supported by a crude administrative structure and undeveloped supply system. A decade of Democratic-Republican hostility to defense spending had taken a toll on the nation's military establishment. No other advantages that the nation might enjoy could overcome that. "The degraded state in which the military institutions have been retained," concluded a Democratic-Republican newspaper "comes now upon us with a dismal sentence of retribution."[12]

1813: America Resumes the Offensive

American officials had reason to believe that the nation would enjoy greater success in 1813 than in 1812. The supply system was somewhat improved, mainly because there had been time to stockpile what was needed for the campaign. In addition, President Madison had made several cabinet changes. Both the new secretary of war, John Armstrong, and the new secretary of the navy, William Jones, were more capable than their lackluster, if not incompetent, predecessors. The U.S Army had gained some experience in 1812 and was growing in both talent and strength. Hull and Van Rensselaer were gone, capable young officers like Pike and Scott were rising to positions of authority, and a generous enlistment bounty had boosted army strength from 12,000 to 30,000. By recruiting locally, the British had also boosted their army strength in Canada, from 10,000 to 20,000, but that still left the United States with a numerical advantage.

U.S. officials were slow to develop their strategy for 1813, but ultimately they followed the same plan for a three-pronged invasion that they had in 1812. The biggest change in American thinking centered on control of the Great Lakes. The British dominated both Ontario and Erie in 1812, and this had enabled them to move men and material freely along the northern border. In fact, command of Lake Erie had played a crucial role in General Brock's capture of Detroit. Officials in Washington planned to make every effort to win control of the lakes both to facilitate the U.S. supply service and to cut British supply lines. "The success of the ensuing Campaign," said the new secretary of the navy, "will depend absolutely upon our superiority on all the Lakes—& every effort & resource must be directed to that object."[13]

The Navy Department appointed 33-year-old Captain Isaac Chauncey to command the lakes. Chauncey took personal charge on Lake Ontario and assigned the command on Lake Erie to 27-year-old Master Commandant Oliver H. Perry. Using a naval yard at Sackets Harbor, New York, Chauncey launched a naval construction program, but the British, whose main yard was only 30 miles away in Kingston, Upper Canada, were able to keep pace. The balance of power on Lake Ontario seesawed back and forth. On Lake Erie, by contrast, Perry built a squadron at Presque Isle (Erie, Pennsylvania) that the British could not match because their own naval yard at Fort Amherstburg was simply too far removed from their sources of supply in the East. As a result, Perry ultimately secured control of Lake Erie. This paved the way for a successful American campaign in the Old Northwest.

When the campaigning season opened in the spring of 1813, the British still controlled Lake Erie and thus held the initiative in the West. Britain's native allies were clamoring for action. Procter, who was now a brigadier general in the British army, was eager to make an assault on Fort Meigs, an Ohio outpost at the rapids of the Miami that Harrison had ordered built under the direction of West Point engineers. An Anglo-Indian assault on Fort Meigs failed, as did a British attack on Fort Stephenson, 30 miles away in present-day Fremont, Ohio. With these failures, Procter called off the campaign and returned to Canada.

By the time that Procter returned to Canada, the balance of power in the region was beginning to shift because of Perry's naval construction program. By September Perry had launched his squadron of ships—headed by two 20-gun brigs, the *Lawrence* and the *Niagara*—from Presque Isle and set sail for South Bass Island at the western end of Lake Erie, where he could cut the British supply line across the lake to Fort Amherstburg. The British squadron, under the command of 26-year-old Commander Robert H. Barclay, was outgunned nearly two to one. Barclay had little choice but to sail from Fort Amherstburg to challenge Perry in order to open up British supply lines. The opposing squadrons met near South Bass Island on September 10. Perry's battle flag was emblazoned with "DON'T GIVE UP THE SHIP," words that had been uttered by a dying Captain James Lawrence several months earlier when his men were about to surrender the U.S. frigate *Chesapeake* to HMS *Shannon*.

In the Battle of Lake Erie, Perry's flagship, the *Lawrence,* took such heavy fire that it was knocked out of action. But instead of surrendering, Perry lowered his battle flag, boarded a boat manned by several seamen, and was rowed to his sister ship *Niagara*. With a fresh ship and crew, Perry returned to the fray and pounded the British ships into submission. Famously, the American commander sent a brief after-action report to General Harrison that read: "We have met the enemy and they are ours: Two Ships, two Brigs, one Schooner & one Sloop."[14]

Perry's victory changed the balance of power in the region. Unable to resupply their troops or native allies on the Detroit River, Procter ordered a withdrawal to the East. Harrison pursued with some 3,000 men, including 1,000 mounted volunteers from Kentucky under the command of a 32-year-old congressional War Hawk and militia officer, Colonel Richard M. Johnson. Harrison caught up with the British and their native allies (about 1,100 men in all) 50 miles east of Detroit and defeated them in the Battle of the Thames on October 5. Johnson was credited, probably correctly, with killing Tecumseh. Kentucky volunteers returned the next day, stripped Tecumseh's corpse of everything, and then cut off strips of his skin to take home as souvenirs. "I [helped] kill Tecumseh and [helped] *skin him*," a veteran of the campaign recalled a half century later, "and brought Two pieces of his yellow hide home with me to my Mother & Sweethearts [children?]."[15]

The victories by Perry and Harrison restored American dominance in the Old Northwest. Although the British still held the post on Mackinac Island and later won control of Prairie du Chen, their power over the Indians had been broken. Most of the native tribes made peace with the United States and either changed sides or sat out the rest of the war. Although native raids continued in the borderlands, the United States had finally won the Indian war that had erupted at Tippecanoe two years before. The British withdrew from western Upper Canada, which became a no-man's-land subject to American raids.

Farther east the United States initially enjoyed success, but in the end a combination of reverses and mismanagement cost the young republic all that it had gained. To strike a blow at British naval power on Lake Ontario, Chauncey ferried a U.S. force to York (now Toronto), home to a small British navy yard. On April 27, the Americans, under the command of Zebulon Pike, who was now a brigadier general, landed west of the main fort and then drove relentlessly to the east. The British, under Major General Roger Sheaffe, the victor at Queenston Heights in 1812, decided to abandon the fort and ordered his men to blow up the magazine, which housed a large quantity of powder. The explosion took place just as the Americans were approaching and took a heavy toll. Among the dead was Pike, who was struck in the forehead by a large stone. Furious over their losses, the Americans looted the town and burned the public buildings. Some locals joined in the looting.

On May 29 the British mounted their own amphibious operation against the U.S. naval yard at Sackets Harbor. Although Prevost was aboard the squadron, Colonel Edward Baynes had operational command. The defense of Sackets Harbor was directed by Lieutenant Colonel Electus Backus of the regular army and Brigadier General Jacob Brown of the New York militia. The invading force took heavy fire, especially from the regulars and a 32-pound gun.

Convinced that all was lost, an American midshipman put the navy yard to the torch, although a hastily organized fire brigade limited the damage by putting out the fire. The British, facing intense fire and concluding that the navy yard (whose destruction was their main goal) was in flames, called off the attack. Backus was among those killed, while Brown was rewarded with a commission as a brigadier general in the regular army.

Sackets Harbor had been left exposed to a waterborne attack when Chauncey's squadron was at the other end of the lake supporting yet another amphibious operation, this time against Fort George at the mouth of the Niagara River. While the British fort was bombarded by Fort Niagara across the river and by Chauncey's squadron from the lake, an American force led by Winfield Scott landed on May 27. Scott's men overran the British force on the shore and occupied Fort George. The British abandoned their positions all along the Niagara River, retreating to the west. Scott started to pursue them, but a cautious New York militia officer who had the overall command ordered Scott to return. The British regrouped in Burlington Heights.

With their army intact, the British defeated an American force not far from Fort George in a night attack at Stoney Creek on June 5–6. This engagement was followed by another British victory at Beaver Dams on June 24. Thereafter, the Americans were bottled up in Fort George, with the British and their native allies maintaining a loose siege. With troop strength in the post steadily declining, the Americans finally abandoned the fort on December 10. Before departing, their commander, Brigadier General George McClure of the New York militia, ordered the nearby town of Newark (now Niagara-on-the-Lake) burned, leaving several hundred people homeless in the winter weather.

Furious over the burning of Newark, the British retaliated. Lieutenant General Gordon Drummond, the 41-year old who was now in charge of that theater, ordered a night attack on Fort Niagara across the river. British troops, relying on their bayonets, captured Fort Niagara on December 19. In the days that followed, the British burned American towns, including Buffalo, all along the Niagara River. "The whole frontier from Lake Ontario to Lake Erie," lamented the governor of New York, "is depopulated & the buildings & Improvements, with a few exceptions, destroyed."[16] A campaign that had begun with such promise at York and Fort George had ended with the British in control of both posts at the mouth of the Niagara (forts George and Niagara) and the American side of the river in flames.

The main reason that Fort George had to be evacuated was that the regulars had been transferred east to take part in the biggest American offensive of the war against Montreal: a double-barreled operation in which Major General James Wilkinson led one army—7,300 strong—from Sackets Harbor down the St. Lawrence River from the west, while Major General Wade Hampton advanced with a second army—3,800 strong—north from Plattsburgh. Neither commander was particularly capable, and because he despised Wilkinson, Hampton refused to cooperate with him. As a result, both armies were defeated, Hampton in the Battle of Châteauguay on October 26 and Wilkinson in the Battle of Crysler's Farm on November 11.

The failed campaign against Montreal brought the fighting to an end in 1813. Although the United States had been successful in the West, subduing most of the native population and reestablishing its ascendancy, this had little impact on the overall course of the war. The theater was simply too far removed from the main centers of Canadian population, commerce, and power. Farther east, the United States again met with failure. After two years of fighting, the United States was no closer to conquering Canada or to forcing the British to yield concessions on the maritime issues.

1814: Britain Invades America

By the time the campaigning season opened in the spring of 1814, the momentum in the war had shifted to the British. The tide in the European war had begun to turn when Napoleon retreated from Russia at the end of 1812, and in the fall of 1813 the allied victory at Leipzig further eroded his dominion over the Continent. While the Duke of Wellington made steady progress in Spain and invaded France from the south, Britain's continental allies rolled into France from the east. By the end of March 1814, allied troops were in Paris. With Napoleon's abdication in April, the war in Europe ended. Already the British had been shifting resources to the American war, and with Napoleon's downfall the flow of men and material to America increased. While U.S. troop strength rose to 40,000 by the spring and 45,000 by the end of the year, British troop strength soared from 30,000 in the spring to over 50,000 by December.

Although the United States was now on the defensive in the East, its logistical advantages in the West enabled it to remain on the offensive. The U.S. plan was to capture Fort Mackinac, establishing undisputed dominion over the West, and to drive the British from the Niagara Peninsula. The British plan was to use their growing strength on land and at sea to invade upper New York, Maine, the Chesapeake, and the Gulf Coast. The mood of the British press was vindictive. "Chastise the savages," said the *Times,* "for such they are, in a much truer sense, than the followers of Tecumseh and the Prophet."[17] But the British government was more interested in seizing territory that could be used as a bargaining chip in the peace negotiations that were scheduled to get under way.

The American offensive in the West met with little success. In June American troops built a fort at Prairie du Chen in what is today Wisconsin but lost it to an Anglo-Indian force in July. A U.S. assault on Fort Mackinac in August also failed. Both posts remained in British hands for the rest of the war and were used as a base for raids by those natives who remained loyal to the Crown. Moreover, the British capture of two U.S. schooners on Lake Huron in September gave them a presence on the lake that allowed them to resupply Fort Mackinac and their native allies.

American raids in the spring on the north shore of Lake Erie took aim at Port Talbot and Dover and met with more success. Colonel John B. Campbell, who oversaw the Dover raid, claimed that the village was infested with "revolutionary tories and half pay officers" who had taken part in the burning of Buffalo the previous December.[18] He used this as an excuse to torch the town. Brigadier General Duncan McArthur led an equally destructive mounted raid 180 miles deep into Upper Canada from Detroit in the fall, burning mills and their storage bins along the way. Denouncing the destruction of private property, British officials were determined to retaliate. This may have played a role in the burning of the public buildings in Washington, D.C., in August.

The United States also took the offensive on the Niagara front, resulting in the bloodiest campaign of the war. In early July Major General Jacob Brown crossed into Canada with an army 5,500 strong. The army included a brigade expertly trained by Brigadier General Winfield Scott, New York and Pennsylvania militia led by Brigadier General Peter B. Porter, and some 500 New York Iroquois led by the aging Seneca chief Red Jacket.

Brown laid siege to Fort Erie, which surrendered after only token resistance. American troops then advanced north along the river road. In early July they defeated the British at Chippawa, fought them to a standstill in the bloody Battle of Lundy's Lane in late July, and then twice successfully defended Fort Erie, first (led by Brigadier General Edmund P. Gaines) against a night attack in August and then (with Brown back in command) against an artillery campaign in September. Although these engagements represented an important milestone in the development of the U.S. Army, the nation had little else to show for the campaign. Because it was not easy to supply from the U.S. side of the river, especially in winter, Fort Erie was blown up and abandoned in early November. Despite all their fighting and heroics, American troops withdrew to the United States, and the British regained control of the Niagara Peninsula.

Farther east the British were closer to their supply centers, and the Royal Navy could bring its power to bear on the American coast. The British had conducted extensive raids in the Chesapeake in 1813, and in 1814 they stepped up the pace, taking aim at larger cities. Their biggest prize was Washington. The northern approach to the city, at Bladensburg, Maryland, was protected by some 6,000 men under the leadership of Brigadier General William Winder, who showed little talent for command or combat. Most of the men were undisciplined militia, but also present were 600 U.S. seamen and Marines under the command of Captain Joshua Barney, who was in charge of an artillery battery of five guns. The British approached with 4,500 men under the command of 48-year-old Major General Robert Ross. Barney's artillery took a heavy toll on the British before the militia protecting his flank gave way and he was overrun. The militiamen were quick to flee from the advancing Redcoats, a retreat that critics dubbed "The Bladensburg Races."

With the road to Washington now open, the British marched in and burned the public buildings, including the Capitol, the White House, and the buildings housing the War, State, and Treasury departments. The superintendent of the Washington Navy Yard, which was the best stocked yard in the nation, added to the conflagration by putting it to the torch to keep the supplies and ships there out of British hands.

The following month the British occupied a hundred miles of the Maine coast. They also raided other parts of New England, often demanding tribute to spare exposed seaports from destruction. In addition, the British seized or destroyed merchant ships and their cargoes, emptied warehouses filled with commodities for export, and burned abandoned farmsteads.

In the Chesapeake, the British presence had the added effect of inciting slaves to seek their freedom. Vice Admiral Sir Alexander Cochrane, the commander of the British fleet on the American station, encouraged this with

The White House in 1814 after the British had torched it. All that remained was a shell, and President James Madison had to set up shop in the Octagon House, which still stands as a Washington landmark. For the United States, the burning of the White House, Capitol, and other public buildings marked the low point of the war. (Engraving of a hand-colored aquatint by William Strickland, Library of Congress)

a proclamation issued on April 2 that promised all interested Americans a "choice of either entering into His Majesty's Sea or Land Forces, or of being sent as FREE Settlers to the British Possessions in North America or the West Indies."[19] More than 4,000 runaway slaves ultimately found sanctuary with the British, and some 550 served in a special Corps of Colonial Marines that took part in the depredations in the Chesapeake. After seeing them in action, Rear Admiral George Cockburn concluded that they made "the best skirmishers possible for the thick Woods of this Country" and that they showed "extraordinary steadiness and good conduct when in action with the Enemy."[20]

Although most of the news in the East was bad in 1814, there were two significant engagements in September that gave Americans cause to rejoice. On the last day of August, Sir George Prevost led an army of 10,000 men into upstate New York to seize territory that could be used as leverage in the peace negotiations. Prevost reached Plattsburgh with 8,000 men and was on the verge of overrunning the American position there when another inland naval defeat threatened his supply lines. Thirty-year-old Master Commandant Thomas Macdonough engineered the U.S. victory on Lake Champlain. Macdonough had set his kedge anchors so that he could rotate his flagship in the midst of the battle to bring a fresh broadside to bear on the opposing British squadron. This proved to be the masterstroke that won the Battle of

Lake Champlain. With the defeat on the lake, Prevost feared his army, even if victorious on land, might be cut off and ordered a withdrawal to Canada.

Americans also celebrated the successful defense of Baltimore. The local militia commander, Major General Samuel Smith, had spent months preparing the defenses of the city. When a British force of 4,500 men landed, he ordered a militia force to block their advance. In the ensuing Battle of North Point on September 12, the British prevailed but suffered heavy casualties. Among the dead was their beloved commander, General Robert Ross, who was killed in a preliminary skirmish. His remains were shipped to Halifax in a cask of spirits for burial.

Ross's successor, Colonel Arthur Brooke, continued the march to Baltimore but was confronted with some 15,000 Americans behind the defensive works that had been erected. The Royal Navy was called upon to soften the American lines, but an extended bombardment of Fort McHenry failed to reduce it, and thus the navy could not get close enough to give Brooke the support he needed. This left the British army with little choice but to abandon its assault on Baltimore.

Francis Scott Key witnessed the bombardment of Fort McHenry from a truce ship under the guns of the main British fleet 9 miles away and celebrated the successful defense of the fort with a song that was subsequently renamed "The Star-Spangled Banner." This popular song became the national anthem in 1931.

Although the successes at Plattsburgh and Baltimore were widely celebrated across the United States, the course of the war was unchanged. The United States remained on the defensive with its resources stretched to the limit and its future in doubt.

The War at Sea

In the first few months of the war, Americans had little to cheer about on the northern frontier, but the war at sea was different. The U.S. frigate *Constitution* performed especially well, outrunning a Royal Navy squadron in a remarkable 57-hour chase that impressed even the British, and then defeating two British frigates, first the *Guerrière* and then the *Java*. In the engagement with the *Guerrière*, British round shot seemed to bounce off the 22-inch hull of the U.S. ship, earning her the nickname "Old Ironsides." The U.S. frigate

President added to the string of victories by defeating the *Macedonian* and bringing the British frigate into port as a prize of war.

The U.S. frigate victories against the Mistress of the Seas went down hard in Britain and gave a huge boost to sagging American morale. At the time, few Americans realized, or acknowledged, that in each battle the American frigate had a decided advantage because it was both bigger and more heavily armed than its opponent. There was no disgrace in losing to a more powerful ship, although defenders of the Royal Navy circulated several myths to explain away the defeats: that the heavy U.S. cruisers were really battleships in disguise and that they had picked crews that were heavily British. None of these claims was true.

Later in the war the British frigate *Shannon* defeated the U.S. frigate *Chesapeake*, and a British squadron defeated the frigate *President*. The victors brought both American ships into British ports as prizes of war. In the end, the British gave as good as they got in the battles on the high seas. Except for proving that the U.S. Navy could go keel to keel with the Royal Navy, there was no clear victor in this phase of the naval war.

As much interest as the naval engagements generated on both sides of the Atlantic, they were strategically unimportant. They had no impact on the course of the war other than inducing the Admiralty to issue a secret order for British frigates not to tangle with the heavy American frigates unless they had help from other ships. More significant was the logistical role performed by the Royal Navy, which moved supplies and later troops across the Atlantic to Canada. No less significant was the blockade that the Royal Navy established along the U.S. coast, targeting the middle and southern states in 1813 and then New England and the Gulf Coast in 1814. The blockade had a crushing impact on the U.S. economy and on federal revenue.

U.S. warships and privateers targeted British trade, forcing the Admiralty to institute a convoy system, which meant that British merchantmen in the Atlantic sailed with an armed escort. The American war on British commerce drove up insurance rates in some waters, most notably the Irish Sea, and elicited a howl of protest from British merchants, who criticized their government for not providing better protection. However, it had little impact on the course of the war. British trade continued unabated. The losses were simply written off as the price of doing business in a war-torn world.

The Crisis of 1814

The U.S. naval triumphs in 1812, the victories by Perry and Harrison in 1813, and the successes on the Niagara and at Plattsburgh and Baltimore in 1814 were worthy of celebration, but they hardly meant that the United States was winning the war. The British remained in the driver's seat, and no one knew whether the United States could escape with its honor, rights, and territory intact.

The military challenges that the young republic faced in 1814 were part of a larger crisis. The British blockade had cut off foreign trade and disrupted the coastal trade. Ships were idled in New England and commodity prices plunged in the South, driving both regions into economic depression and leading to growing discontent.

With their normal peacetime economic activities disrupted, Americans looked for other ways to make a living. The nation's land and water frontier was long and exposed, and British commissary agents had plenty of money to buy food and whatever else they needed. Everywhere cash-strapped Americans were willing to supply their needs. In 1813 the Lexington *Reporter* complained "that the very squadrons of the enemy now annoying our coast . . . derive their supplies from the very country which is the theater of their atrocities."[21] The flow of American food across the Canadian border, where a large and growing British army menaced the nation, was even more scandalous. "Two-thirds of the army in Canada," boasted Sir George Prevost in August 1814, "are at this moment eating beef provided by American contractors, drawn principally from the States of Vermont and New York."[22]

The loss of normal commercial opportunities not only encouraged Americans to trade with the enemy but also deprived the government of much-needed income at a time of soaring war costs. Government revenue, which was heavily dependent on foreign trade, was an anemic $11 million in 1814, while government expenses had risen to nearly $35 million. The Treasury proved unable to float a war loan that summer and as a result had to rely heavily on Treasury notes, a kind of interest-bearing paper money that had first been issued in 1812. It now flooded the market and depreciated in value. Most banks, many of which were already insolvent, refused to take Treasury notes. Only the neediest of government contractors would accept them.

The lack of funds made it difficult to pay for the war or to meet other government obligations. The secretary of navy reported that his department was "destitute of money in all quarters" and that he had no funds for even "the most urgent contingent purposes."[23] Army recruiting came to a standstill in some districts, militia mutinied for want of pay, and the desertion rate among regulars climbed. Government officials could not afford to care for prisoners of war or to purchase medical supplies for troops in combat zones, and the armory in Springfield, Massachusetts, had to suspend operations. The Treasury was so short of funds that in the fall of 1814 it defaulted on the national debt. By all indications, the nation was on the brink of financial collapse.

Compounding the growing crisis was the refusal of the administration's opponents to support the war effort. Some Federalists in the fall of 1814 talked about supporting the war, but nothing came of it. The administration was unwilling to give up its designs on Canada or to take any Federalists into the cabinet, and Democratic-Republicans in Congress showed little inclination to seek common ground with their traditional foes. To Federalists the war never lost its partisan character. To them it looked like the war remained a war of conquest and that Democratic-Republican leaders had no interest in forming a government of national unity to meet the crisis.

In New England, where Federalist opposition was the greatest, there was talk of pulling out of the Union and signing a separate peace. By the fall Federalists in this region had called for a convention to meet in Hartford to air their grievances. With some New England newspapers openly discussing secession, many feared the worst. "There is not a state in Europe," claimed the Russian ambassador, "which, in similar circumstances, would not have been considered on the eve of revolution."[24] Fortunately for the nation, moderates controlled the Hartford Convention, and the report they issued in January 1815 avoided any talk of secession.

Adding to the crisis atmosphere were the terms laid down by the British when the two sides opened peace talks in August. By then the United States had abandoned any hope of winning concessions on the maritime issues and simply wanted peace. But the British, eager to exploit the military advantage they now enjoyed, sought concessions to win greater security for Canada and their native allies. As their price for peace, the British demanded that the United States surrender territory in northern Maine and Minnesota; agree to the creation of a huge Indian reservation in the Midwest; remove all warships and dismantle all military posts on the Great Lakes; and give up traditional fishing privileges in Canadian waters. When these terms were published in

America in October, there was widespread consternation. Everyone realized that if the British did not relent the war could go on indefinitely.

Encouraging Signs

The crisis that the United States faced in 1814 was worse than anything it had experienced since the American Revolution. The fate of the nation hung in the balance. And yet, as low as the morale of the nation had sunk in the summer of 1814, there were encouraging signs, even at this dark moment.

The most important sign came from the British people. However much they might want to punish the United States and impose a favorable peace, they were weary of war. After all, the British had been at war with France for nearly 20 years when the war with America erupted. If Britain's armed forces did not deliver success on the battlefield quickly, the desire to end the war taxes and all the burdens associated with waging war might well trump the hope for a clear and decisive victory.

Several other developments also worked to America's advantage. First of all, the successful defense of Plattsburgh and Baltimore showed how difficult it was to mount offensive operations far removed from one's sources of supply, especially in the North American wilderness. Secondly, the United States was now blessed with an experienced and disciplined army, one that had been transformed into an effective fighting force by its combat experience, particularly on the Niagara front. Especially noteworthy was the quality of officers who had risen to important positions in the army: William Henry Harrison and Duncan McArthur in the West; Jacob Brown, Winfield Scott, and Edmund Gaines on the Niagara; and a host of lesser officers in just about every theater. All had shown that they had what it took to manage successful operations. The defense of the young republic was now in their hands.

Harrison's services ended when he resigned in disgust in 1814 in response to open hostility from Secretary of War John Armstrong. The vacant major generalship was filled by another warrior from the borderlands who would leave an even greater mark: Andrew Jackson, a transformative figure whose astonishing success in the Southwest and on the Gulf Coast would have a decisive impact on how the War of 1812 passed into American history.

2 The Making of a Hero

ANDREW JACKSON was the product of the rough Carolina back-country. He lost his entire family early in life and had to scramble to rise above his modest origins. He also had to migrate to the West, where life could be tough, dangerous, and uncultured, but where opportunity abounded.

Alone in the Carolinas

Jackson was born in the Waxhaw Settlement in South Carolina in 1767. Two years earlier, his Scotch-Irish parents had migrated to America from northern Ireland. The family was poor and had trouble making a living off the farmland they worked. Any hope that young Jackson would enjoy a normal childhood perished two weeks before his birth when his father died, leaving his mother with three young boys—Hugh, Robert, and Andrew—to care for. She left her eldest, Hugh, with a relative and moved the rest of her family into her invalid sister's home, where she served as housekeeper.

Jackson's education was modest, and he quit school at the age of 13 to serve in the American Revolution. His older brother Hugh had already died in the service, probably from disease. The two remaining Jackson brothers took an active part in the war, and young Andrew got a full taste of all of its bloody horrors. The Jackson brothers were at the Battle of Hanging Rock in South Carolina, a hotly contested engagement in 1780 that was typical of the vicious skirmishing in the South. Andrew's exact role is unknown, but given his age, it is likely that he remained out of sight with the horses.

Jackson and his brother continued to take part in partisan warfare in the region until they were captured by the British and imprisoned in Camden, South Carolina. When a British officer ordered Jackson to clean his boots, the willful boy refused. The officer struck him with a sword, and Jackson carried the resulting scars as well as a sizeable dent in his skull for the rest of his life. More than six decades later he described the experience: "The sword point," he recalled, "reached my head and has left a mark there as durable as the skull as well as on the fingers."[1] Jackson's brother also refused the officer's demand and received a more serious head wound.

Jackson and his brother were exchanged for British prisoners, but before being released both contracted smallpox. Although Jackson survived, his recovery took months. His brother was not so fortunate, dying from a combination of smallpox and the festering head wound received from the British officer. Jackson's mother also died in 1781—probably of typhus or cholera—while nursing captured Americans on a British prison ship in Charleston Harbor. With her death, Jackson, only 14, found himself alone in the world.

Jackson never forgot his mistreatment during the war and blamed the loss of his family on the British. His life was long and fruitful, but he never quite got over his resentment against the former mother country. Years later, on the eve of his campaign on the Gulf Coast that would culminate in the Battle of New Orleans, Jackson confided to his wife, "I owe to Britain a debt of retaliatory Vengeance."[2] His enmity was not only personal but also ideological. He regarded Britain as a land of corruption and oppression. In 1798, when it appeared that France might invade England, he said: "Should Bonaparte make a landing on the English shore, Tyranny will be Humbled, a throne crushed and a republic will spring from the wreck." As a result, "millions of distressed people" would be restored to their rights.[3]

At the end of the Revolutionary War, Jackson lived with relatives, bouncing from job to job (including a stint as a teacher) and living a life of dissipation punctuated by bouts of depression. He was not entirely without means, having inherited from his mother a 200-acre farm and probably some other assets that could be turned into cash. But he went through whatever money he had quickly and sold the farm in 1792 after he had moved west.

In 1784 Jackson decided to study law. At the time there were no law schools in the nation. The first, Judge Tapping Reeve's Litchfield Law School, was just then being established in Connecticut, and it would be attended mainly by affluent young men from New England. Most aspiring lawyers simply apprenticed themselves to an established lawyer and "read" (that is, studied) law in his office. They transcribed documents, ran errands, and performed other duties in exchange for an opportunity to read legal treatises and learn what the law was and how it was applied. Jackson read law in Salisbury, North Carolina, first with Spruce McCay and then with Colonel John Stokes.

Jackson spent his evenings with other young men in Salisbury, drinking, gambling, and blowing off steam in athletic contests and games. He was also fond of juvenile pranks and emerged as something of a leader in these dubious activities. According to one source, he had a well-deserved reputation as the "most roaring, rollicking, game-cocking, horse-racing, card-playing, mischievous fellow that ever lived in Salisbury."[4]

By the fall of 1787 Jackson had learned enough law to launch his own practice. He appeared before the superior court of North Carolina, and after an oral examination, the judges pronounced him morally fit and knowledgeable enough to practice law in the state. He spent the next six months doing minor legal work and weighing his options. If Jackson had been part of an established family or had other local connections that he could exploit, he might have remained in this part of North Carolina. But without those advantages, his prospects were limited, and the West beckoned.

The American West

The U.S. West in the 1780s stretched from the Appalachian Mountains in the east to the Mississippi River in the west and from the Great Lakes in the north to Spanish Florida in the south. Seven of the 13 colonies had overlapping claims to this territory prior to the American Revolution, but during that conflict the region was largely a no-man's-land. Control over key areas shifted back and forth depending on the latest success of the British, American, or native war parties that were operating in the region. Even the most successful expeditions, such as George Rogers Clark's into the Illinois country in 1778–79, did not secure the territory. American claims to the West were still unsettled when the peace negotiations got under way in Paris in 1782, and it took some shrewd maneuvering to ensure that all of this territory was awarded to the United States in the Treaty of Paris in 1783.

The American peace delegation—John Adams, Benjamin Franklin, and John Jay—was charged with winning independence and (if possible) securing the Mississippi River as the western boundary of the United States. But Spanish officials, eager to keep land-hungry Americans as far away as possible from their own colonies west of the Mississippi, sought to fix the boundary much farther east. Not only were the French willing to go along with this, but they even suggested that the British might retain much of the territory north of the Ohio River. Facing the prospect of losing more than half of the West, the American envoys decided to seek a better deal by opening bilateral negotiations with the British even though this violated their instructions from the U.S. government as well as the terms of the Franco-American Treaty of Alliance. The British, eager to undermine the alliance and to keep any disputed territory out of the hands of their traditional European enemies, willingly agreed to fix the U.S. boundary at the Mississippi River.

Although the United States got the boundaries it wanted, its hold over this vast territory (which was 42 percent of the nation's landmass) was far from secure. As of 1790, fewer than 200,000 of the nation's 4 million people lived in the region, and although Americans were pouring in from the East, the situation remained dynamic. In the south, the Spanish disputed the boundary until 1795 and until 1803 controlled the lower Mississippi River, which was the most important outlet for western commodities. In the north, the British occupied eight forts inside of U.S. territory until 1796. Both European nations also maintained relations with Indians living in the West. The British even called for the creation of a native buffer state in the Old Northwest.

Few Indians in the West were happy to be under U.S. jurisdiction, and American encroachments on their lands only added to their resentment. Small settlements were subject to attack, isolated farmsteads were even more vulnerable, and those planning a journey were wise to arm themselves and travel in groups. Adding to the uncertainty, some Americans in the West schemed to acquire vast tracts of land, launch new states, invade Spanish territory, or secede from the Union. Such were the differences between the safe and sedate East and the rough settlements beyond the Appalachian Mountains that for all practical purposes they were two different worlds. Those living in the West acknowledged as much by proudly referring to their region as the "Western World."

The Confederation government faced three pressing challenges in the West in the 1780s: to establish local governments, to devise a land policy, and to pacify the native population. The states with western claims gradually surrendered them to the national government, and the Confederation Congress responded with two ordinances: the Land Ordinance of 1785, which provided for surveying and selling lands in the West; and the Northwest Ordinance of 1787, which established a process for organizing territories that would eventually join the Union as states. But federal action to implement these laws lagged behind western demands, and the Indians did not make peace until the 1790s. Hence, the West remained a place of danger and uncertainty. In spite of these liabilities, the region was filled with opportunities for those adventuresome enough to risk moving there. The land was fertile and well watered, and lawyers like Andrew Jackson were in demand to help fix land titles, collect debts, and settle other disputes.

A New Home in the West

Jackson's opportunity to move west came in early 1788 when he was promised a job as public prosecutor in the western district of North Carolina, which later became Tennessee. This was not a full-time job, but it would help a struggling young lawyer make ends meet. That spring Jackson followed the Wilderness Trace across the Appalachian Mountains with a group of friends to Jonesborough. Several months later he was part of a larger group that pushed 275 miles farther west over the newly opened Old Road or Avery Trace to the budding young settlement of Nashville on the Cumberland River. The settlement was only 8 years old and had nearly been wiped out by several Chickamauga raids, but thereafter it enjoyed rapid growth. By 1810 Nashville boasted a population of 1,100; two years later it became the state capital.

Besides launching what quickly blossomed into an impressive law practice in Nashville, Jackson developed an extensive trading business, shipping commodities (mostly cotton) down the Mississippi River to Natchez and New Orleans and purchasing merchandise (such as clothing and other dry goods) in Philadelphia for resale in the West. Jackson took an oath of allegiance to the Spanish Crown in 1789. This was essential for anyone wanting to do business in Natchez or New Orleans, both of which were in Spanish territory.

A contemporary described Jackson as "a cool shrewd man of business," but in the 1790s he nearly landed in debtor's prison.[5] He had taken part in the national passion for land speculation, sometimes buying or selling tens of thousands of acres at a time. When he endorsed the notes (equivalent to modern checks) that a Philadelphia merchant named David Allison had issued, he found himself responsible for the notes when Allison went bankrupt. The sum involved was staggering. Years later Jackson put its value, with interest, at $20,000. Jackson had to sell much of his property to cover the obligation. This experience made him more cautious in his commercial dealings, and he sought to avoid debt altogether.

To serve his clients, Jackson sometimes had to travel, occasionally to places as far away as Jonesborough. The trips could be dangerous because Creeks, Cherokees, Chickamaugas, and Shawnees still claimed much of the land, and they usually did not welcome intruders. John Donelson, one of the founders of Nashville, was killed by Indians while surveying. Jackson periodically went on punitive expeditions with militia that targeted Indians who had raided their settlements.

In 1791 Jackson started living with Rachel Donelson Robards, John Donelson's daughter, who was eager to trade her wretched first husband for someone who was truly in love with her and treated her better. They may have married at this time, although no documentation exists to support such a claim. The young couple was unaware that a report that Rachel's husband had secured a divorce was untrue. Several years later, when he did secure a divorce, the couple formally married, perhaps for the second time.

Jackson's enemies made much of his irregular domestic arrangement over the ensuing 30 years, claiming that he had run off with another man's wife. This caused Jackson much anguish and led to several duels. "He was most prompt to defend his wife's good name," claimed an early biographer. "For the man who dared breathe her name except in honor, he kept pistols in perfect condition for thirty-seven years."[6] By all accounts the match was a good one. Jackson reaped considerable benefit from marrying into a prominent Virginia family that had played a central role in the founding of Nashville, and Rachel did essential service by managing their estate during Jackson's many long absences.

Success in Private and Public Life

Despite his humble origins and his close call with bankruptcy in the 1790s, Jackson prospered from his various enterprises, and it did not take long for him to become part of the local Tennessee elite. By the mid-1790s he had given up his law practice and cultivated an upper-crust agrarian lifestyle. He began purchasing land and in 1804 acquired an estate he called the Hermitage. He also raised and raced horses. He bought his first slave in 1788, owned 15 by 1798, and claimed 95 by the time he became president in 1829.

Unlike some members of Virginia's landholding aristocracy, Jackson had no second thoughts about slavery. On occasion he traded in slaves, and he punished those who tried to run away by selling them, typically "down the river" to the deep south. No less revealing was a newspaper ad that he ran in 1804, offering $50 for the return of a runaway "and ten dollars extra, for every hundred lashes any person will give him, to the amount of three hundred [lashes]."[7]

In 1790 North Carolina ceded her western territory to the United States, and it was organized into the Southwest Territory. Tennessee was carved out of this territory and joined the Union as a state in 1796. The party rivalries that characterized politics in the East did not develop in the Southwest where just about everyone was a Democratic-Republican. Instead, politics in Tennessee revolved around personalities and factions. At issue were not the great policy questions that divided Federalists and Republicans but rather who would control state offices and thus the power and patronage that went with them.

As a member of the dominant local faction headed by the influential territorial governor, William Blount, Jackson's star rose, and he held a number of territorial offices. After Tennessee joined the Union, he was elected to the House of Representatives as the state's sole congressman but resigned after one session when he was elevated to the U.S. Senate. Although he was careful to look after the interests of his constituents, the cosmopolitan capital city of Philadelphia held no great attraction for him, and he had little patience with the seemingly endless debates in Congress. He also preferred to be with Rachel and closer to his business interests, especially after Allison's failure nearly bankrupted him. "I have Experienced more disquietude in a political life," he told a friend in 1798, "than all the advantages derived from it can compensate for and I assure you that my political life will be a short one."[8] True to his word, Jackson resigned his Senate seat after just one session.

Jackson also served six years, from 1798 to 1804, as a judge on the state's highest court, where he developed a reputation for delivering justice that was swift and fair. On one occasion, he cleared 50 cases in 15 days. He did such a commendable job that a large number of prominent citizens petitioned him to remain on the bench longer than he had planned.

The public position that Jackson coveted most, however, was a major generalship in the Tennessee militia. The choice was up to the field officers in the division, and Jackson had sought the post as early as 1796, when it went to a client of Governor John "Nolichucky Jack" Sevier, a popular Revolutionary War hero and famous Indian fighter. Jackson finally got the position in 1802, but only after Governor Archibald Roane (who was a Jackson ally) cast a tie-breaking vote for him over Sevier. Jackson was the only major general in the militia for about 18 months, when the Tennessee legislature divided the militia into two divisions, creating a second major generalship. Jackson headed only the western division, although he remained the senior major general.

Jackson's military experience was modest, limited mostly to his Revolutionary War experience as a youth and the Indian expeditions he had taken part in. His new position was no sinecure. Situated in the western borderlands, Tennessee had recurring problems with the native population, so citizen soldiers were called into service far more often than were their eastern counterparts. Jackson's election as a major general was as much a political choice as anything else, but no doubt many of the senior officers in the division saw in him a man with a talent for leadership.

Jackson had another quality that most westerners probably considered essential to his new military position: an abiding hostility and distrust of Indians. Native raids on settlements or attacks on U.S. troops sent him into a nearly apoplectic rage in which he called for a war of extermination. After the Indians in the Old Northwest had attacked General Harrison's force at Tippecanoe in late 1811, Jackson told Harrison: "The *blood of our murdered Countrymen must be revenged*—That banditti ought to be swept from the face of the earth."[9] Six months later, after a Creek raid on the Duck River, he told the Tennessee governor: "We must . . . carry fire and sword to the heart of the Creek Nation, and to learn these wretches in their own Towns and villages what it is to massacre Women and Children at a moment of profound peace."[10]

Jackson deeply resented the federal government's failure to protect these settlements when Tennessee was still a territory. He was invariably a proponent of punishing wayward Indians, stripping them of their lands, and forcing them to move further west. All of this foreshadowed his policies during the Creek War and much later when he was president.

Controversy and Intrigue

In 1801 James Wilkinson, the commanding general of the U.S. Army, issued a general order requiring all members of the service to cut their hair short. In the French Revolution, long hair—typically worn in a braid hanging from the back of the head—was considered a badge of aristocracy. Wilkinson could not have chosen a better way to ingratiate himself with the new Democratic-Republican administration in Washington and to serve notice on the largely Federalist officer corps that a new regime had come to power. There was considerable grumbling among the officers, but the only one who refused to comply was Colonel Thomas Butler, the second highest-ranking man in the service and one who had amassed an impressive record of service in peace and in war. Butler claimed that the order was illegal because it violated his personal rights. He was twice court-martialed and ultimately suspended from the service, but he died before the suspension could be carried out and was buried with his cherished locks intact.

Andrew Jackson, who had long been Butler's friend, sported long hair himself (although not in a braid). He wrote to President Jefferson on Butler's behalf, and when he got no satisfaction, he orchestrated a public protest from the militia in Tennessee asking Congress to set Wilkinson's order aside. This also failed to generate any action. Jackson's very public attack on Wilkinson and defense of Butler did not endear him to the administration.

Jackson alienated the administration even more with his actions during the Burr Conspiracy. In 1805 former vice president Aaron Burr toured the West. As the first prominent national statesman to visit the region, he received a warm welcome. That he had killed Federalist Alexander Hamilton in a duel the year before hurt his reputation in the East but not in the West, where dueling was accepted and Hamilton's immensely unpopular whiskey tax had only recently been repealed. In Nashville, Burr's welcome was especially warm because he had championed Tennessee statehood in 1796. Jackson attended a public dinner on his behalf and entertained Burr at the Hermitage. Burr was trying to line up support for his western conspiracy, and he evidently told people what he thought they wanted to hear. While to some he spoke of detaching the West from the Union and creating a new nation, he told Jackson that his aim was to seize Spanish territory that would be annexed to the United States.

Jackson endorsed Burr's plan and, at the latter's request, ordered boats built and provisions stockpiled. At the same time, one of Jackson's young friends raised a company of volunteers to accompany Burr down the Cumberland, Ohio, and Mississippi rivers to New Orleans. Jackson was stunned to learn that the government believed that Burr was guilty of treason and had ordered his arrest. Summoned to Richmond to testify before a grand jury, Jackson continued to defend Burr after the New Yorker had been formally charged. Jackson considered Wilkinson the real criminal and was convinced that the government was going after the wrong man. In fact, Wilkinson had been Burr's co-conspirator before turning state's evidence. He was also suspected (correctly, as it turned out) of being on the payroll of the Spanish government.

Jackson remained in Richmond for Burr's trial. He publicly attacked Wilkinson, who was the government's star witness, calling him "a Spanish hireling."[11] Jackson, who had been steaming ever since the death of Butler, wrote a long and insulting letter to Secretary of War Henry Dearborn, denouncing him for supporting Wilkinson's persecution of Butler and accusing him of "the most notorious & criminal acts of dishonor, dishonesty, want of candor & justice" in connection with his handling of the Burr Conspiracy.[12]

Brawls and Duels

Like many southerners and westerners, Jackson was quick to resent insults and engage in duels or brawls. In a society that lacked a titled aristocracy, defending one's honor was one of the few ways that a man could show that he was a gentleman. And for a man like Jackson, who had not been born into gentility, the need to demonstrate that he truly belonged to society's upper crust was even more compelling. Thus for Jackson issuing a challenge was more than a matter of protecting his reputation from slander and demonstrating his courage and manhood: "My reputation is dearer to me than life," he told one antagonist. "For malicious slander," he told another, "all men are answerable at the bar of honor."[13] But a gentleman dueled only with other gentlemen. The way to secure satisfaction for an insult from someone who was not a gentleman was to cane or horsewhip him.

Soon after arriving in Jonesborough, Jackson found himself in a courtroom facing an accomplished lawyer named Waightstill Avery, who ridiculed his young opponent's knowledge of the law. In response, Jackson challenged Avery to a duel. "My character you have Injured," he wrote Avery, "and further you have Insulted me in the presence of a court and a large audience. I therefore call upon you as a gentleman to give me Satisfaction for the Same."[14] At the ensuing meeting on the field of honor, both men evidently shot into the air, throwing their fire away. Jackson declared that honor had been satisfied, and this ended the matter.

In 1803 Jackson (who was a state judge) and rival John Sevier (who was governor) nearly came to blows outside a courthouse in Knoxville. Jackson had accused Sevier (correctly) of land fraud, and Sevier accused Jackson of running off with another man's wife. Furious, Jackson challenged Sevier to a duel, but the governor declined because Tennessee had outlawed dueling in 1801. Jackson responded by publicly branding Sevier "a base coward and a poltroon" who "will basely insult, but has not courage to repair the wound."[15] Sevier's reputation survived the insult, but the two men remained bitter enemies.

In 1806, when a dispute arose over the settlement of a horse racing bet, Jackson caned Thomas Swann, claiming there was no proof that the young man was a gentleman and thus entitled to a duel. Jackson blamed the dispute on Swann's friend, Charles Dickinson, who responded by challenging Jackson to a duel. The duelists agreed to meet across the Kentucky state line, where dueling was still legal. Dickinson was considered a crack shot, the best in Tennessee. Jackson decided that his best chance was to give his antagonist first fire and then carefully take aim himself. Dickinson fired first and appeared to miss. Jackson then took deadly aim and delivered a mortal wound to Dickinson. Jackson walked some distance from the field when a doctor who was with him noticed that one of his shoes was filled with blood. Jackson had been wearing a large coat over his thin frame, and Dickinson's aim was slightly off, his shot just missing Jackson's heart. Jackson survived the ordeal but carried Dickinson's pistol ball in his breast for the rest of his life.

Seven years later Jackson feuded with the Benton brothers, Thomas Hart and Jesse. With his friend John Coffee, Jackson confronted the brothers on

September 4, 1813, at the City Hotel in Nashville. The ensuing brawl, which Thomas Hart Benton called "the most outrageous affray ever witnessed in a civilized country," was waged with pistols and knives and ultimately embroiled six or eight people (accounts differ).[16] It is a wonder that no one was killed. The Benton brothers sustained various knife wounds, while Jackson was wounded by Jesse Benton, who had fired a double-shotted pistol. One ball shattered Jackson's left shoulder, the other lodged in his left arm.

Jackson was carried to the Nashville Inn, where he lost so much blood that he soaked two mattresses. Physicians wanted to amputate, but Jackson demurred and ultimately recovered with his arm intact, although the ball remained in his shoulder. The wound refused to heal properly and troubled Jackson until the ball was finally removed nearly 20 years later. Jackson's duels and brawls did him little credit. Although they demonstrated his courage, they also showed a ferocious temper, and the wounds pained him for the rest of his life.

Woodcut depicting Jackson's brawl with the Benton brothers, Jesse and Thomas Hart, in 1813. The quarrel began when Jackson felt obligated to support a protégé whom Jesse Benton had challenged to a duel. Jackson figures prominently in the middle of the fracas, which a later campaign biographer believed important enough to include in a book recommending Jackson for the presidency—such an honorable, rough-and-tumble fellow deserved the vote of every good American. (Jack Downing, *The Life of Andrew Jackson, President of the United States* [Philadelphia, 1834], Library of Congress)

Jackson's Character and Future

By 1807 Jackson's violent controversies had made him a number of enemies. Sevier and Dickinson were popular men, and by insulting the former and killing the latter Jackson alienated contemporaries. Many now considered Jackson "a violent, arbitrary, overbearing, passionate man."[17] Democratic-Republican leaders in Washington had no better opinion of the outspoken and violent westerner who was so often critical of them. Jefferson later said of Jackson that "his passions are terrible . . . he is a dangerous man," and Madison was slow to call for his services during the War of 1812.[18]

Jackson spent the years from 1807 to 1812 mostly on his estate, his influence diminished but still significant. By this time both his appearance and personality were firmly fixed. He had sandy hair and deep blue eyes and was gaunt, measuring 6 feet 1 inch in height and weighing about 140 pounds. He was a skillful horseman and an excellent shot. Unlike the leading Democratic-Republicans of the day—Jefferson and Madison and many of their friends—Jackson was more a man of action than of ideas. He was not given to abstract thinking and was direct and blunt rather than cautious and tactful.

Jackson could be impetuous and hot-tempered, exploding ferociously at anyone who defied or insulted him, even in a minor way. He was ever loyal to his friends but showed unbridled hostility to his enemies. Yet some friends, like John C. Calhoun, might later become enemies, and some enemies, like Thomas Hart Benton, later became friends.

Above all, Jackson had character traits that made him so often successful. He was scrupulously honest, had a commanding presence, radiated authority, showed undaunted courage, and was blessed with an invincible will. Whatever resistance or obstacle he faced, he refused to accept defeat or failure. As a result, in the end he usually got what he wanted.

Jackson might have spent the rest of his life at the Hermitage had the War of 1812 and the Creek War not intervened to create a demand for his military services. For 15 months beginning in late 1813, he actively campaigned against the nation's enemies. Those 15 months fundamentally transformed his life and had a profound impact on the future of the nation.

3 The Creek War

ANDREW JACKSON was 45 years old when the War of 1812 began. Like most Democratic-Republicans, he supported the decision to go to war to vindicate the nation's sovereignty and uphold its maritime rights. Even though Jackson was preeminently a man of the West who blamed Indian raids on the British, this was not a major consideration in his support for the declaration of war. For Democratic-Republicans in the West as well as the East, the war was undertaken mainly to uphold "Free Trade and Sailors' Rights." Jackson laid out the case in a message to his militia division on the eve of the war:

> We are going to fight for the reestablishment of our national character, misunderstood and vilified at home and abroad; for the protection of our maritime citizens, impressed on board British ships of war and compelled to fight the battles of our enemies against ourselves; to vindicate our right to a free trade, and open a market for the productions of our soil, now perishing in our hands, because the *mistress of the ocean* has forbid us to carry them to any foreign nation; in fine, to seek some indemnity for past injuries, some security against future aggressions, by the conquest of all the British dominions upon the continent of North America.[1]

"Old Hickory" Is Born

Once war was declared, Jackson was eager to mount a campaign. He wrote to President Madison offering to raise 2,500 volunteers to fight the British. But there was little appetite in Washington for calling on this outspoken westerner who had been so unrestrained in his criticism of the administration. In any case, Tennessee was too far south to conveniently supply troops for any offensive against Canada, so volunteer militia from Kentucky, Ohio, and New York were recruited to support the regular units that were sent north. Moreover, instead of offering the inexperienced Jackson a command, the War Department selected one of his subordinates, James Winchester, to be a brigadier general in the U.S. Army. Winchester had served as a junior officer in the American Revolution, and Jackson considered him a "brave and good" man. However, he proved unequal to his command and surrendered his entire army in early 1813 at the Battle of Frenchtown.[2] The notorious River Raisin massacre ensued the next day.

Jackson finally got his chance at the end of 1812 when the War Department ordered him to lead 1,500 men, who were designated U.S. Volunteers, from Nashville to New Orleans to reinforce Major General James Wilkinson in the Crescent City. Jackson had been sharply and publicly critical of Wilkinson during the Burr Conspiracy trial in 1807. Nevertheless, his command, at least for now, was independent, and he set aside his animosity to put the nation first. "It is a bitter pill to have to act with him," he told a friend in Washington, "but for my country's good I will swallow [it.] I go with the true Spirit of a Soldier—to defend my country and to fight her battles."[3]

Wilkinson was widely distrusted in Tennessee, and it was a bitterly cold winter, with a foot of snow on the ground in Nashville. Yet there was no shortage of volunteers. Nearly 2,100 men arrived at the rendezvous point on December 10, 1812. This gave Jackson a force that was a third larger than the War Department had called for. In preparing for the campaign, Jackson first encountered problems that were to bedevil him throughout the war: supply and pay problems and mutiny. Jackson was eager to march but lingered in Nashville waiting for food, munitions, and other supplies.

Pay for Jackson's men was not forthcoming, which produced considerable discontent and sparked a small mutiny. Americans who volunteered for military service in this era—whether as state or federal volunteers—considered themselves under contract. If the government failed to live up to the contract, particularly in matters of pay and rations, the men no longer felt obligated to perform their duties. To quell this incipient mutiny, Jackson relied on the influence of his officers. He also ordered the pertinent provision on mutiny in the Articles of War read to the men, a provision that explicitly authorized the death penalty for mutineers. This was just the first of a series of mutinies that Jackson faced in the war. His men often took a very different view of their military obligations than he did. Some would later get a hard lesson on just how unbending their commanding general could be.

Jackson finally left Nashville on January 7, 1813, moving most of his men by boat down the river system, while his mounted troops traveled overland. He was slowed by sheets of ice in the rivers, and one of his boats and the supplies it carried sank, but by mid-February he had reached Natchez, where he marked time awaiting further orders. Jackson maintained a good camp, and his men responded to his leadership. According to one officer, "With such a commander at our head as our beloved Jackson (so I will term him, for he is loved by all), *any* troops would behave well."[4]

A month after arriving in Natchez, Jackson received orders from Secretary of War John Armstrong to abandon his mission and dismiss his troops. In effect, Jackson was being ordered to turn his troops loose (including the sick) without pay, without food and other vital supplies, and without any way of returning home 500 miles away through dangerous Indian country.

Jackson was livid. "The history of all *Barbarous Europe*," he said of Armstrong's order, "cannot furnish a parallel."[5] Jackson refused to abandon his men to their fate. He was already purchasing medical supplies with his own money, and now he covered the cost (for which he was later reimbursed) of marching his men home. It took a heroic effort to keep the demoralized troops in line, and Jackson showed considerable care for the men during the march.

There were not enough wagons to carry all of the sick, and Jackson, who was racked with dysentery (as he was throughout the war), refused to ride any of the three horses he brought with him. Instead, he insisted that the horses of all the officers be reserved for those who were too sick to walk. Jackson's determination to overcome all obstacles to complete the journey was clear to everyone. His men compared him to hickory, one of the hardest woods in the West, and soon the affectionate nickname "Old Hickory" was born. The heroic march back to Tennessee produced more than just a nickname. It also demonstrated Jackson's effectiveness as a leader.

Jackson's men appreciated his leadership. So, too, did other people in Tennessee who heard tales of the march. "Long will their General live in the memory of his volunteers," said the Nashville *Whig*, "for his benevolence, humane, and fatherly treatment to his soldiers."[6] Reports of Jackson's march even reached the nation's capital, and there were rumors that he might be in line for a commission in the regular army. Although Jackson repeatedly indicated his interest in serving on the Canadian frontier, nothing came of it. When he got another chance, it was not to fight the British on the northern border but to protect Tennessee's southern flank from a large band of militant Creeks.

Border Warfare

The Creek War (also known as the Red Stick War) was just one chapter in the long, sordid history of conflict between settlers and natives in North America. Although land was at the root of most of the trouble, a dehumanizing viciousness on both sides fueled the hatred. Revenge killings were an accepted way of securing justice and settling accounts in the culture of many Indian tribes, and noncombatants, including women and children, were not spared. In addition, the natives took scalps, sometimes from victims who were still alive, and while they might adopt prisoners of war to replace fallen braves, they were more likely to torture and kill them. But settlers, particularly Americans, could be equally brutal. They indiscriminately killed or tortured innocent natives, proudly displaying the scalps they took and rarely taking prisoners. There was no real law in the borderlands; both sides saw nothing wrong in what they did.

In the mid-1790s, the French observer, the Duke de La Rochefoucauld, toured North America and reported on the relationship of settlers and Indians living in the southern borderlands. "It is admitted by everybody," he said, "that there cannot be a more vicious set of people than the whites who dwell on the boundaries: they rob, murder, and betray the Indians; who in return frequently destroy their persecutors, together with their families."[7] Reports of atrocities by settlers rarely made the press, while those committed by natives almost always did.

Americans had little understanding of the plight of the Indians or of the reasons that might induce them to go on the warpath. Most Americans (especially Democratic-Republicans and particularly those in the West) attributed native uprisings to the bloodlust and savagery of the Indians or to the nefarious influence of British or Spanish agents. But it was a U.S. agent who precipitated the Indian War in the Old Northwest in 1811. Acting with the full support and approval of President Thomas Jefferson, Governor William Henry Harrison had imposed a series of outrageous land cession treaties on the native population. This had led to the outbreak of war at Tippecanoe.

When the Indian War in the Northwest came to an end with the American victory at the Thames in 1813, Thomas Jefferson, now in retirement, blandly remarked, "This unfortunate race, whom we had been taking so much pains to save and to civilize, have by their unexpected desertion and ferocious barbarities justified extermination, and now await our decision on their fate."[8] *Niles' Register* made a similar point about the Creeks, claiming that the United States had treated them "with the utmost gentleness and generosity" and that they had "no possible cause of complaint."[9] Hezekiah Niles, who published his magazine in Baltimore, was more than 750 miles from Creek country and had little understanding of the native people he was referring to.

The Transformation of Creek Society

The Creeks, also known as Muskogees, claimed much of present-day Alabama and Georgia but were bunched mainly in towns along two rivers. The Upper Creeks lived on the Tallapoosa River and the Lower Creeks on the Chattahoochee River. The Creeks were neighbors to the Cherokees, Chickasaws, Choctaws, and Seminoles. These tribes were later known as the Five Civilized Tribes because by the early nineteenth century they had embraced so many of the American settlers' ways.

In traditional Creek society, the men hunted, fished, and made war, while the women managed the family home (which belonged to them) and were responsible for preparing food, making clothes, and caring for the young and old. Both genders cooperated to maintain small subsistence farms. The men were often gone or kept to themselves, and with such sharply defined gender roles, men and women even spoke slightly different dialects.

The traditional way of life began to erode almost as soon as the Creeks came into contact with Europeans. Contact with the Spanish unleashed fatal diseases, which had a devastating impact. From 1500 to 1700, the Creek population may have declined by as much as 95 percent, from perhaps 200,000 to 10,000. Although the population more than doubled in the eighteenth century, the Creek nation remained but a shadow of its former self. As a result of contact, Creeks also became dependent on Europeans (mainly the British) for manufactured goods, especially cloth, axes, knives, guns, ammunition, powder, and liquor. To pay for the goods, Creeks had to greatly increase the time they spent hunting to get deerskins and furs. They also raided other tribes for captives that could be sold as slaves in Charleston and other eastern markets.

The influx of European goods and the emergence of an Anglo-Creek nexus of trade gradually undermined traditional gender roles. Moreover, as settlers and their growing herds of cattle encroached upon Creek lands, game—already overhunted—became even more scarce. The Creeks found themselves without the pelts they needed to trade for what they wanted (often rum or whiskey) or what they needed (the manufactured goods they had come to depend upon). As a result, Creek indebtedness to European traders became the norm.

Some mestizos (that is, mixed bloods) were already adopting European ways by 1760. After the American Revolution U.S. officials urged all Creeks to embrace commercial agriculture and other aspects of American life to survive the decline of game. Among those who had already taken this path was Alexander McGillivray (1750–93), a mestizo who spent most of his youth apprenticed to Scottish merchants in Charleston. McGillivray established a plantation in Creek country, and as a wealthy and literate mestizo with powerful friends in the United States and Spanish Florida, he spearheaded the drive to establish a new order in Creek society. But in his dealings with U.S. and Spanish officials to impose the new order, McGillivray always pursued his own interests first, occasionally accepting bribes and deceiving his fellow Creeks.

Some Creeks (mostly mestizos) willingly followed McGillivray's lead, embracing the new social order and pursuing profits at the expense of the tribe. Although not all gave up hunting, they were willing to farm and raise livestock. The women, in turn, cultivated cotton and took up spinning and weaving. In addition to new gender roles, these Creek embraced the concept of private property, sought to accumulate wealth, and promoted literacy and education. They even embraced that quintessential symbol of the caste system in southern society, slavery, even though at one time Creeks had considered the institution alien and had routinely offered sanctuary to runaway slaves. Emblematic of their new way of life, Creek converts began to fence in their property, lock up their valuables, and brand their livestock. Forsaking the practice of burying a dead man's possessions with him, they also began to pass on their wealth to their heirs.

This transformation was already well under way in 1796 when Benjamin Hawkins was appointed Indian agent in the Southwest, a position he held until his death in 1816. Hawkins established his agency on the Flint River in western Georgia. Traveling extensively in Creek country, he forged close ties with the mestizos who embraced his "plan of civilization." Using the resources of his office, he put key chiefs on his payroll and funneled annuities to compliant towns.

Especially important was Hawkins's success in 1798 in endowing the ancient Creek National Council with legislative and executive authority and with police power to enforce the law. The National Council could now punish those who defied its will and could even order the execution of those who broke the law. This undermined the traditional influence of the family and the clans. The older system that had relied on persuasion was replaced with a new one that rested on coercion. It also heightened competition and exacerbated conflict between the Upper and Lower towns.

By 1812 the mestizo Creeks had adopted so many of the defining values and conventions of Americans that they had come close to achieving the U.S. goal of assimilation. The principal American aim in fostering assimilation was to meet the appetite of land-hungry settlers by freeing up the vast hunting grounds that the native population claimed. This pressure was relentless. As soon as tribal leaders agreed to a new boundary, American squatters moved beyond the line, creating a demand for the acquisition of still more territory. However cooperative and "civilized" the Creeks might be, they could do little to slow the unyielding pressure to surrender ever more territory to their American neighbors.

Revolt of the Red Sticks

Just as the loss of their lands and the erosion of traditional values elicited a vigorous backlash among Indians in the Old Northwest, there was a growing restlessness among the Creeks in the Old Southwest. Especially unhappy were the young men in the Upper Towns, who depended on combat to earn their reputations and on the hunt for their livelihood. A long period of famine that began in 1804 emboldened them because it highlighted the growing

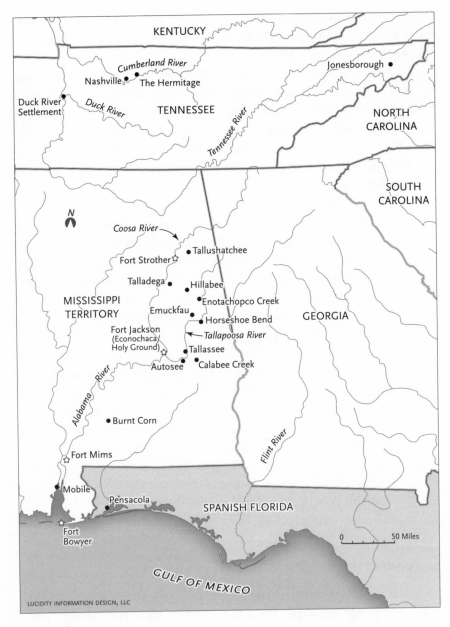

The Creek War

gap between the few (almost all mestizos) at the top of the new social order, who had plenty to eat and lived in relative comfort, and the many at the bottom, for whom starvation was a real and constant danger. The U.S. construction of roads through Creek country in 1811–12 added to their discontent.

Like the militants in the Old Northwest, dissident Creeks could see their lands, their livelihood, and their way of life slipping away and were determined to reverse the trend. Native prophets who rose up in their midst urged them on. In late 1811, Tecumseh (who was part Creek) visited the southern tribes, urging them to resist further American encroachments. While he won little support from most of the tribes, the militant Creeks were receptive to his message. They were known as "Red Sticks" because they painted their war clubs (which resembled hatchets) red, indicating that they were ready for war.

In 1812 the Red Sticks became increasingly hostile to the settlers. As a result the borderlands became unsafe. In May a small war party headed by Little Warrior raided a farmstead on the Duck River southwest of Nashville, kidnapping Martha Crawley and brutally killing seven other people who were present, including five children. Although Crawley ultimately escaped and made her way home, the Duck River Massacre, as it was called, was luridly described in the press and created consternation in Tennessee. It was well known that Tecumseh had visited the Creeks, and it was widely believed that he and other British agents were trying to stir up a native war in the southern borderlands.

Across Tennessee there were demands for reprisals. Breathing fire, Andrew Jackson told the governor that he wanted to march an army into the heart of Creek country and insist on justice "at the Point of a Bayonet." Until Martha Crawley and her captors were surrendered, he said, "[I] think myself Justifiable in laying waste their villages, burning their houses, killing their warriors, and leading into Captivity their wives and Children." Jackson's old nemesis, John Sevier, who was now a member of Congress, agreed. "Fire and sword," he said, "must be carried into that country before those wretches will be reduced to reason or become peaceful neighbors." Doubtless, he added, "British emissaries are among them."[10]

The Duck River Massacre was followed by another widely publicized attack in February 1813. Little Warrior and a band of Red Sticks had journeyed north to visit Tecumseh in the Old Northwest. In January 1813, they took part in the Battle of Frenchtown and the ensuing River Raisin Massacre. On their way home, they attacked a small settlement in Kentucky, killing its residents. This increased the demand for U.S. retaliation.

Much to the dismay of Jackson and other Tennesseans who demanded swift military action, the War Department decided instead to ask Benjamin Hawkins to seek punishment of the militants through the Creek National Council. Fearful that the militants might provoke war with the United States, the Council ordered Little Warrior and the other Red Sticks responsible for the string of raids to be hunted down. Little Warrior was killed resisting arrest in April 1813, and six of his followers were executed.

The death of the Little Warrior and his followers infuriated other Red Sticks. Tension had been steadily building between the National Creeks, who favored accommodation and assimilation, and the Red Sticks, who were determined to make a stand against further encroachments on their lands. The killing of Little Warrior and the other Red Sticks led to open war between the two groups. The Red Sticks attacked the National Creeks, burning their homes and destroying their livestock, spinning wheels, and other symbols of assimilation. By the middle of 1813, the Red Sticks had gained the upper hand, persuading or compelling most of the Creek villages to embrace their cause and forcing the National Creeks to flee to the safety of the U.S. Indian agent. As part of their campaign, the Red Sticks also stepped up their raids on American settlements across the southern borderlands.

Burnt Corn and Fort Mims

In July 1813, after several raids in the Mississippi Territory, a band of Red Sticks visited Spanish Florida to secure goods and munitions. The Spanish cultivated the Creeks as a counter to their aggressive U.S. neighbors to the north but had no desire to provoke an American war. On July 27, some 80 Indians led by mestizo Peter McQueen were en route home with their goods when they camped about 80 miles north of Pensacola on Burnt Corn Creek. Discovered by American spies, the camp was attacked by 180 Mississippi militia and volunteers consisting of Americans and mestizos led by Colonel James Caller. In the ensuing desultory three-hour engagement—known as the Battle of Burnt Corn—casualties were light. Although the Americans and their mestizo allies made off with most of the goods, the Red Sticks, who had driven off a much larger force, considered the battle a victory and were emboldened to seek out other targets.

The Battle of Burnt Corn was the opening salvo in the Creek War. It transformed what had been a civil war in Creek country into a much larger and more destructive war with the United States, a war that proved disastrous to the entire Creek nation. It also intensified the Creek civil war and drew other native tribes into the conflict. Besides the National Creeks, U.S. agents successfully recruited Cherokees, Choctaws, and Chickasaws as allies.

A month after Burnt Corn, the Red Sticks attacked Fort Mims, a wooden stockaded enclave some 40 miles north of Mobile. The fort was manned by 140 militia under the command of Major Daniel Beasley. Another 250 Americans and mestizos had taken refuge in the fort to escape Red Stick raids. Beasley took his duties lightly and did not prepare adequately for the possibility of an attack. On August 29, two slaves working outside the fort reported seeing Indians lurking nearby. An alarm was sounded, and mounted soldiers were sent to investigate, but when they found no sign of the natives, Beasley ordered the slaves whipped.

The following day, more than 700 Red Sticks launched a full-scale assault on the fort, catching the garrison by surprise. The gate to the fort could not be closed because blown dirt had piled up against it. When Beasley tried to close it, he became the first defender to fall. The fighting was vicious and costly to both sides. The principal Red Stick leader, a Scottish-Cherokee mestizo named William Weatherford, tried to restrain the Indians when they got the upper hand but failed. "My warriors were like famished wolves," he said, "and the first taste of blood made their appetites insatiable."[11] The Red Sticks lost at least 100 killed and many more wounded, but they killed more than 250 of the defenders, including many civilians. The Indians also took upwards of 100 captives, mostly women and slaves. Around 50 survivors, some badly wounded, managed to escape into the wilderness.

The American casualties were bad enough, but early reports that circulated in the West exaggerated them and, as the governor of Louisiana put it, "spread consternation through the Territory."[12] "Our settlement is overrun," added a judge in the Mississippi Territory, "and our country, I fear, is on the eve of being depopulated."[13] Known as the Fort Mims Massacre, this engagement stirred up people throughout the Old Southwest much as the River Raisin Massacre had in the Old Northwest.

The U.S. Response

The demand for retaliation was nearly universal, and westerners were quick to respond to the call. Throughout the region militia units were called into service and volunteers were recruited to guard the borderlands and undertake punitive expeditions. The ensuing U.S. operations were dogged by recurring supply, enlistment, and discipline problems. In addition, with several armies operating across two military districts, there was little cooperation and considerable confusion.

Despite these liabilities, Americans had a number of significant advantages: Their military leadership was superior to the Red Sticks'; also, their armies were much larger and had better weapons. (A shortage of rifles and muskets forced many Red Sticks to rely on the bow and arrow.) The Americans also received indispensable assistance from their Creek, Choctaw, Cherokee, and Chickasaw allies. These allies not only conducted independent operations against the Red Sticks, but they swelled U.S. numbers on the battlefield and performed vital services by scouting and tracking the enemy. Without this native assistance, the course of the war might have been very different.

U.S. operations in Creek country began in earnest in the fall of 1813. In the Mississippi Territory, Captain Sam Dale, known as "Big Sam" to the Indians, had been wounded in the Battle of Burnt Corn but had recovered enough to return to the field. Determined to drive out the native war parties preying on U.S. settlements, he led a force of 40 men up the Alabama River, reaching what is today Monroe County, Alabama. On November 12, in a legendary skirmish known as the Canoe Fight, Dale boarded a large Indian dugout and killed several Red Sticks in hand-to-hand combat. Dale's daring and courage gave people in the territory both a victory to celebrate and a hero to honor.

Six weeks later a much larger operation was launched from the Mississippi Territory. At the head of a mixed force of 1,000 regulars, militia, volunteers, and Choctaws, Brigadier General Ferdinand L. Claiborne targeted Econochaca, also known as the Holy Ground, the home of William Weatherford, which was located on the Alabama River in present-day Lowndes County, Alabama. Claiborne attacked on December 23. After some hard fighting, the Red Sticks fled into the wilderness. The last to leave was Weatherford, who escaped in what was long known in western lore as "Weatherford's Leap." Facing sure capture, he rode his horse off a bluff, leaping into the Alabama

River 15–20 feet below. He popped up in the water, still holding the reins of his horse, made it to the opposite shore, and rode off into the wilderness. Claiborne's men burned the Red Stick village and another one nearby, destroying or carrying off all the provisions and property they found.

Red Stick strongholds were also targeted from Georgia. Brigadier General John Floyd took aim on Autosee, a large Creek village inhabited by around 1,000 warriors and their families. With 1,000 Georgia troops and 300–400 National Creeks led by William McIntosh, Floyd attacked Autosee on November 29. Floyd used his field artillery followed by a bayonet charge to drive off the native warriors and then burned Autosee as well as the nearby village of Tallassee. Floyd and his Indian allies sustained about 75 casualties (including Floyd, who was severely wounded). An estimated 200 Red Sticks were killed, many perishing when the buildings they had taken refuge in were burned.

In January 1814, Floyd, who had recovered enough from his wounds to return to the field, again marched into Creek country, this time with 1,200 Georgia troops, some cavalry, and 400 National Creeks. Floyd's army camped on Calabee Creek, and in the early morning hours of January 27, a large Red Stick force attacked. The fighting was fierce, and Floyd's camp was nearly overrun, but a combination of artillery and rifle fire followed by a bayonet charge drove the natives off. Although Floyd's men retained control of the field, the Battle of Calabee Creek was a Red Stick victory. The Red Sticks suffered only 50 dead and an unknown number wounded. Floyd's men sustained around 170 casualties and were so demoralized that Floyd ended the campaign.

Jackson Enters the War

The operations launched from the Mississippi Territory and Georgia took a heavy toll on the Red Sticks but were far from conclusive. The campaign from Tennessee, by contrast, was decisive, mainly because it was led by Jackson, who refused to quit until he had achieved complete victory. By the fall of 1813 Jackson had assembled 2,500 men to undertake an expedition into Creek country. The force consisted of the U.S. Volunteers raised in 1812 who were recalled into service and volunteer militia from Jackson's West Tennessee division.

Among those present was 27-year-old Davy Crockett. Immensely popular with the other men, Crockett "was there with his rifle and hunting-shirt, the merriest of the merry, keeping the camp alive with his quaint conceits and marvelous narratives."[14] Jackson was in great pain, still recovering from wounds suffered just weeks before in his brawl with the Benton brothers, but "Old Hickory" was determined to assume command and to wipe out the Red Sticks. "The blood of our women & children," he told his troops, "shall not call for vengeance in vain."[15]

Jackson marched his army south to the Coosa River, where he built Fort Strother as a supply base and prepared for battle. In a public address, Jackson urged his men to ignore the war whoops of the enemy that so often panicked inexperienced and experienced troops alike and to be ready for close-in combat. "Great reliance," he said, "will be placed by the enemy on the consternation they may be able to spread through our ranks by the hideous yells with which they commence their battles; but brave men will laugh at such efforts to alarm them. It is not by bellowings and screams that the wounds of death are inflicted. You will teach these noisy assailants how weak are their weapons of warfare by opposing them with the bayonet; what Indian ever withstood its charge? what army of any nation ever withstood it long?"[16]

Tallushatchee and Talladega

On November 3, 1813, Jackson's friend and lieutenant Brigadier General John Coffee led 900 mounted Tennessee militia and volunteers and some National Creeks and Cherokees against the Red Stick village of Tallushatchee. Using tactics pioneered by Hannibal 2,000 years before, Coffee formed his men into a semicircle around the village. When the Red Sticks attacked, he closed the loop. Coffee sustained fewer than 50 casualties in the Battle of Tallushatchee, while the Red Sticks suffered at least 200 killed and 84 women and children captured. "The enemy fought with savage fury," Coffee reported, "and met death with all its horrors without shrinking or complaining: not one asked to be spared, but fought as long as they could stand or sit."[17] Nearly 50 of the natives made their final stand from inside a house. According to Davy Crockett, "We now shot them like dogs; and then set the house on fire, and burned it up with forty-six warriors in it."[18]

A native baby boy whose mother was killed in the battle survived the attack. When none of the Indian women would care for him, Jackson took charge of the boy. Jackson named him Lyncoya and raised him at the Hermitage. Jackson had no biological children but took several children into his home. He hoped to send the boy to the U.S. Military Academy, but when Lyncoya was 16, he contracted consumption (tuberculosis) and died.

Several days after Coffee's victory, Jackson learned that 1,100 Red Sticks were besieging a stockaded town of National Creeks at Talladega. Jackson marched 2,000 men to the town and on November 9 used the same tactics as Coffee to envelop the Red Sticks. The natives suffered huge casualties, leaving 300 dead on the field, before finding a weak spot in Jackson's line and escaping. Jackson lost only about 100 men killed or wounded. The National Creeks inside the town, who were desperately short of water, welcomed Jackson as their savior. Although the Battle of Talladega was a clear U.S. victory, the escape of the Red Sticks meant that the Creek War would continue.

Shortly after that battle, the Hillabee Creeks, who had fought Jackson there, offered through a friendly Scottish trader to lay down their arms. Jackson was amenable, but word of the initiative failed to reach the other American armies in the region. Shortly after Jackson's response reached the Hillabees, they were attacked by a force of East Tennessee troops and Cherokees under Brigadier General James White. Taken by surprise and expecting peace, the Hillabees offered virtually no resistance. White's men killed 64 warriors and took over 250 prisoners (mostly women and children) while sustaining no losses themselves. Not surprisingly, those Hillabees who escaped fought to the bitter end, and thereafter few other Red Sticks bands considered surrender an option.

U.S. Supply and Discipline Problems

After the Battle of Talladega, Jackson was so low on food that he had to return to Fort Strother. "We were out of provisions and half starved for many days," he told his wife.[19] Supply was a recurring problem that most field commanders faced, and Jackson was no exception. Even before the first battle of the campaign, Jackson was worried about keeping his men fed. "There *is* an enemy," he said, "whom I dread much more than I do the hostile Creeks. . . . I mean the meager monster, FAMINE."[20] He blamed government contractors, who frequently chiseled on the quality or quantity of the provisions they supplied or failed to deliver altogether. "All the difficulties & delays of the Campaign," Jackson complained, "are to be ascribed, primarily, to the negligence of the Contractors."[21] The lack of food demoralized the troops and made them unwilling to stay beyond their enlistment periods.

Expiring enlistments nearly destroyed Jackson's army. "Great discontent prevails in all our camps," wrote Brigadier General John Coffee. "The men appear to have turned their faces towards home, and nothing can induce them to stay."[22] Militia units were usually called out for three months and volunteers for whatever term they had agreed to, which ranged from 60 days to a year. But how long militia had been called out for was sometimes a matter of dispute, and Jackson claimed that if no term were specified he could hold the men in service for the duration of the war. Also subject to debate was the question of whether the clock on the one-year volunteers enlisted in late 1812 continued to run when they were at home between campaigns. If, as the men insisted, it did (which the language of the law seems to suggest), they could go home on December 10, 1813.

Convinced that one more campaign would end the Creek War, Jackson interpreted the law so as to keep his army intact and considered all other interpretations mutinous. On occasion he threatened volunteers with militia or militia with volunteers. Jackson's left arm was still in a sling from his confrontation with the Bentons, but he faced down nearly a whole brigade by resting his musket on the neck of his horse and threatening to shoot the first man who moved. On another occasion Jackson ordered artillerymen to hold lit matches over loaded cannon aimed at men planning to leave. Jackson himself was in the line of fire, but this only illustrated his determination. "The manner, appearance, and language of General Jackson on occasions like this," commented an early biographer, "were literally *terrific*. Few common men could stand before the ferocity of his aspect and the violence of his words."[23]

Back home, the governor's faith in the campaign was beginning to flag. He suggested that Jackson give up and return to Tennessee. In a long and emotional letter, Jackson sought to buttress the governor's resolve. "Your country is in danger," he pleaded. "Apply its resources to its defense. Can any course be more plain?"[24] With support waning in the field and at home, Jackson's indomitable will was the only thing that kept the campaign alive.

Jackson's officers sided with their men, and the War Department later ruled in their favor. In the end Jackson could not stop his volunteers and militia from returning home, although he continued to grouse about it. "The once brave and patriotic Volunteers," he complained, had been reduced to "mere whining, complaining, seditioniers and mutineers," and the militia were "risking all the penalties of desertion, sedition and mutiny." The departure of the troops, he added, "may destroy the campaign and leave our

Jackson single-handedly puts down a mutiny of Tennessee volunteers. Amos Kendall—an influential Kentucky newspaperman and ardent Jackson supporter— published this etching in 1843 or 1844 to celebrate Jackson's courage and resolve. (Library of Congress)

frontier again exposed to the Tomahawk of the ruthless savage."[25] The volunteers and militia who left camp, in turn, spread stories in Tennessee of Jackson's excessive drinking (which was not true) and of his angry and arbitrary rule (which was).

Emuckfau and Enotachopco Creek

Jackson's determination stiffened the backbone of the governor, who authorized 2,500 fresh volunteers for three months of service. By mid-January 1814 reinforcements had arrived in Jackson's camp, bringing his strength back to about 1,000 men, although most were raw recruits. Resuming the offensive, Jackson marched his army, which included Cherokees and National Creeks, into the heart of Red Stick country where he fought two defensive battles, both of which were fiercely contested.

Camping at Emuckfau on January 21, Jackson sent out spies, who reported that the Red Sticks were three miles away and (given their dancing) probably preparing to attack. Jackson was ready the next morning when the Red Sticks attacked his camp from three directions. The attacks were not well coordinated, which enabled Jackson to focus on each attack as it occurred. For their main attack, the native warriors took cover behind trees and fallen logs and repeatedly fired into the American camp. Jackson finally drove them off with a frontal charge. Coffee was wounded in the Battle of Emuckfau, and Jackson's brother-in-law was killed.

Jackson realized that his weakened army of raw recruits was now in considerable danger and ordered a withdrawal. The Red Sticks followed, and on January 24, as Jackson's army was crossing Enotachopco Creek, the natives attacked. Jackson ordered his rear to hold while his left and right wings recrossed the river to encircle the Indians. But much to his chagrin, the troops in his rear echelon panicked and, following their officers, fled into the creek. Only with great difficulty was Jackson able to halt the panic, regain control of the men, and launch a successful counterattack that scattered the Red Sticks.

Jackson's composure during the Battle of Enotachopco Creek was remarkable. According to his aide, Major John Reid, the commanding general was "firm and energetic, and at the same time perfectly self-possessed. . . . In the midst of showers of balls, of which he seemed unmindful, he was seen performing the duties of subordinate officers, rallying the alarmed, halting them in their flight, forming his columns, and inspiriting them by his example."[26] Davy Crockett, who called their escape a "tight squeeze," gave much of the credit for turning the rout into victory to Colonel William Carroll (a future governor of Tennessee). He thought that Jackson "was nearer whipped this time than he was at any other" in the entire war.[27]

In the two battles, Jackson suffered about 100 casualties, the Red Sticks perhaps twice this number. Jackson was convinced that the second battle would have ended in a decisive victory had the men in his rear not panicked. He did not blame the men for following their officers but had no sympathy for the latter. "They ought to be shot," he said laconically.[28] Instead, one was dismissed from the service. By this time the Red Sticks had taken note of their extraordinary foe and given him a pair of nicknames, "Sharp Knife" and "Pointed Arrow."

The Execution of John Wood

Jackson withdrew to Fort Strother, where he waited for the arrival of fresh troops. His success in the field had garnered considerable attention in

Tennessee, which helped recruiting. By February 1814 his army had grown to 4,000 men. Particularly important was the arrival of 600 regulars, whom Jackson believed would give "strength to my arm & quell mutiny."[29]

Jackson continued to worry about the reliability of his independent-minded troops, and to instill discipline he made extensive use of military courts, targeting not just common soldiers but officers as well. "The disorder that prevailed amongst officers & men in our late excursion," he said, "was a striking example and a sufficient warning never to enter the country of our enemy with troops not reduced to some kind of obedience & order."[30]

Especially controversial was Jackson's treatment of a young soldier from his own division. Private John Wood (or Woods), 18 years old, refused to obey orders and, with musket in hand, continued to be defiant even after he was confronted by officers. When Jackson learned of Wood's recalcitrance, he burst from his tent, shouting, "Which is the [damned] rascal? Shoot him! shoot him! Blow ten balls through the [damned] villain's body!"[31] By this time Wood had calmed down and given up his gun, but Jackson, mistakenly thinking that this was Wood's second offense, decided to make an example of him.

Wood was court-martialed. On March 11 he was convicted of mutiny, disobedience of orders, and showing disrespect to a commanding officer. The court recommended that he be shot, but no one—except Jackson—thought that the sentence would ever be carried out. Convinced that Wood showed "an incorrigible disposition of heart" and "a rebellious and obstinate temper of mind," Jackson approved the sentence. It was carried out three days later before his entire army—the first execution of a citizen soldier since the Revolution. "An army cannot exist where order & subordination are wholly disregarded," Jackson said in defense of his actions.[32]

The rest of Jackson's men took the lesson to heart. Militiamen, who heretofore had assumed they could not be executed for any offense, now realized they could. According to a contemporary source, "a strict obedience afterwards characterized the army."[33] Jackson got a lot out of his men, not only because he was an inspiring leader but also because the troops feared him as much as they feared the enemy.

Horseshoe Bend and Fort Jackson

Jackson learned from his native allies that about 1,000 Red Sticks had established a camp 75 miles south of Fort Strother. The camp was on a 100-acre

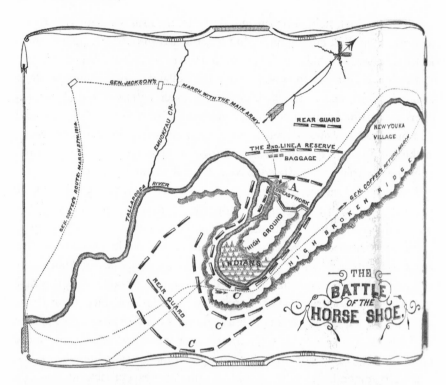

In the Battle of Horseshoe Bend, Jackson's main force stormed the Red Sticks' breastworks from the front, while General John Coffee and allied Indians cut off their retreat and threatened their rear. (Benson J. Lossing, *Pictorial Field-Book of the War of 1812* [New York, 1868])

wooded peninsula called Horseshoe Bend on the Tallapoosa River. The Red Sticks had fortified the neck of the peninsula with large timbers, stacked 5- to 8-feet high and pierced with a double row of gun ports that would enable the defenders to cut down anyone who approached from any angle. The Indians had canoes stashed at the river's edge to escape downriver or across the water into the wilderness if their defenses were overrun.

Jackson led a large army of around 3,000 men (including a sizeable force of National Creeks and Cherokees) to the Red Stick encampment. When he got near, he dispatched John Coffee across the river with a detachment of soldiers and Indians to threaten the Creeks from the rear. At 10:30 a.m. on March 27, 1814, he launched his attack. While Coffee's Cherokee allies swam across the river and made off with the Red Stick canoes, Jackson opened fire at the top of the U with two small fieldpieces and rifles and muskets.

Jackson made little impression on the heavy breastworks. When he realized that some of Coffee's men (mostly Cherokees) had used the Creek canoes to re-cross the river and attack from the rear, he ordered a frontal assault. Among the first over the breastworks was a junior regular army officer, 21-year-old Sam Houston, who took an arrow in his thigh. Houston ordered a fellow officer to yank the arrow out, and once his wound was bandaged he returned to the fray. "The Raven" was wounded twice more in the battle but survived to become the sixth governor of Tennessee in 1827 and then the first president of the independent Republic of Texas in 1836.

Once Jackson's men got over the breastworks, the battle turned into a slaughter. The "*carnage*," Jackson told his wife, "was *dreadful*."[34] Almost without exception, the Red Sticks preferred death to surrender, and those who tried to escape were shot down. The killing dragged into the night and then resumed the next day. When Jackson tried to get some Indians who had taken refuge in a cave on a river bluff to surrender, they responded with gunfire. These Creeks were finally flushed out by lighting the underbrush on fire, and they were shot down as they emerged from the cave. Among those fighting to the bitter end were the Hillabees.

Nearly 800 Red Sticks perished in the Battle of Horseshoe Bend, while Jackson's own killed and wounded numbered only 200. To get an accurate count of the Creek dead, Jackson's men cut off the tips of their noses. Some soldiers also stripped skin off the native corpses to make bridle reins or made off with other souvenirs from their fallen foes.

From Horseshoe Bend, Jackson marched deeper into Creek country to the Hickory Ground, the geographic center and sacred meeting place of the Creek nation. This place was supposedly protected by deities. Creeks believed that no white man could violate it without suffering death. Jackson pointedly challenged this myth and asserted U.S. power by rebuilding an old French post located there and renaming it Fort Jackson. His victory over the Red Sticks was now nearly complete. "The fiends of the Tallapoosa," Jackson triumphantly announced, "will no longer murder our women & children, or disturb the quiet of our borders."[35]

The Battle of Horseshoe Bend broke the back of Red Stick resistance. Most of the Red Sticks, including the leading chiefs, surrendered. Although William Weatherford had taken part in the Fort Mims massacre and other battles, he was not present at Horseshoe Bend. But with the Red Stick defeat in that battle, he had had enough, and he marched into Jackson's camp to surrender. "My people are no more!!" he said. "Their bones are bleaching on the plains of Tallushatchee, Talladega, and Emuckfau."[36] Although many westerners thought Weatherford's role in the Fort Mims Massacre merited death, Jackson was impressed by his foe's candor and bravery and spared him. Weatherford became an emissary for peace, urging other Red Sticks still in the region to give up. Weatherford lived out his days as an affluent and respected planter in Monroe County, Alabama.

Some Red Sticks refused to surrender and instead fled to Florida, intent on joining the Seminoles. Not all made it safely to Seminole country. In August 1814 Jackson dispatched over 1,000 mounted men (including some Choctaws) under Major Uriah Blue to ferret out the refugees. Blue scoured the swamps and waterways of West Florida, seeking out the hiding places of the Red Sticks. He captured many and killed those who resisted. This was the final campaign of the war.

The Creeks sustained over 3,000 dead in the war. This was roughly 15 percent of their population. The destruction wrought by the war left many members of the tribe, friend and former foe alike, dependent on the United States for food. By the summer of 1814, the United States was supplying rations to more than 8,000 Creeks.

In the peace negotiations that followed, the Creeks had no leverage, no way of resisting Jackson, who demanded a huge land cession, ostensibly to cover the cost of war. The National Creeks pleaded that their lands be spared and even offered Jackson a large tract (9 square miles, nearly 6,000 acres) to be located anywhere in the ceded lands in the hope of softening his position. But Jackson was adamant. He left the decision on the gift up to Congress (which never approved it) and refused to budge on his territorial demands.

The Treaty of Fort Jackson, signed on August 9, 1814, stripped the Creeks of 33,000 square miles (over 21 million acres), which was more than half their territory. It also banned any Creek contact with the British or Spanish and guaranteed the U.S. right to establish forts and trading posts and to build roads in Creek country. Only one Red Stick leader was present to sign. The other 30 leaders forced to sign on behalf of 35 Creek bands were all allies of the United States.

Jackson had used the Creek War as a pretext to seize a huge expanse of Indian country. Such an immense landgrab was popular in the West but left officials in Washington aghast. The Senate did not approve the treaty until six months later—only after news had arrived of Jackson's great victory at New

Orleans. When news of that "unparalleled victory" reached Washington, said a U.S. senator, "all opposition to that treaty . . . subsided."[37] The Treaty of Fort Jackson all but destroyed the Creek nation. It set the stage for future land cessions and for the forced removal of Indians to the West that Jackson carried out during his presidency.

The Consequences of Victory

Jackson's victories brought peace to the Southwest and solidified U.S. control over the region. With the defeat of the Red Sticks, it was no longer necessary to maintain a military force on the southern border. And with the region secure, any U.S. force operating on the Gulf Coast did not have to worry about threats to its rear or disruption of its supply lines. The campaign also provided crucial combat experience to Jackson's officers and men that would serve them well on the Gulf Coast. Jackson's victory over the Red Sticks, in other words, played an indispensable role in setting up the successful military operations that followed against the Spanish and British.

Jackson had demonstrated that he was a superb field commander who could overcome obstacles that most other military leaders would find insurmountable. Although there were still some complaints in Tennessee about his command style, his success in the field trumped everything. The West had given the nation a military hero. Jackson was favorably compared to William Henry Harrison, who had a larger and better supplied army and did far less campaigning over a much longer period of time. Even the followers of John Sevier in Tennessee now showered praise on Old Hickory.

Jackson's victories established his reputation far beyond Tennessee. Other than Harrison, who had combined with Oliver H. Perry to restore U.S. dominance in the Old Northwest, as of the spring of 1814 the West had produced few national heroes. The naval heroes who had bested the British on the high seas were celebrated, but their victories had had little impact on the course of the war. As someone who had subdued the entire Southwest, Jackson was embraced by Democratic-Republicans everywhere.

Newspapers around the nation carried Jackson's after-action reports in full, and western members of Congress pressured the administration to give him a regular army commission. Major General Thomas Pinckney, who ranked second only to Henry Dearborn in the U.S. Army chain of command, concurred. As the ranking officer in the South, he had received a steady stream of reports on Jackson's successful campaigns. He lauded Jackson's "intelligent bravery and good conduct," telling the secretary of war that without his "personal firmness, popularity, and exertions . . . the Indian war, on the part of Tennessee, would have been abandoned, at least for a time."[38] No one, he added, was more deserving of a high command in the regular army.

The administration agreed with Pinckney. When William Henry Harrison resigned from the army, the War Department offered his major generalship to Jackson, who accepted on June 18. Jackson was now the ranking officer in the Seventh Military District, which included Tennessee, Louisiana, and the Mississippi Territory. Despite the public accolades that Jackson received, however, there was still some reluctance, at least in Congress, to according Old Hickory the credit he deserved. Some eastern congressmen dismissed his victories because they came against "*mere* savages."[39] A congressional resolution adopted on November 3, 1814, that praised the gallantry of six senior U.S. officers in the field mentioned only those who had recently distinguished themselves on the Niagara front. Jackson's name was nowhere to be found in the resolution.

Shortly after signing the Treaty of Fort Jackson, the new major general departed from Indian country for the Gulf Coast. Sailing down the Alabama River, he arrived at Mobile on August 22. This set the stage for the greatest triumph of his life, a victory that made him the most popular man in the nation and that for generations to come fixed the public memory of the war.

The British on the Gulf Coast

THE WAR of 1812 could only be won (or lost) on the Canadian-American frontier. To have any chance of victory, the United States had to seize and hold a large part of Canada. What the British would have done if the new nation had attained this objective is anyone's guess. Weary from more than 20 years of nearly continuous warfare with France, they might simply have accepted the loss and made peace. More likely, they would have bided their time until the war in Europe was over and then dispatched a large army from the Continent to retake the lost territory. However, they would not have given up impressment to recover that territory. Surrendering this practice would have led to wholesale desertions from the Royal Navy into the American merchant marine. This, in turn, would have undermined British naval power and put at risk Britain's prosperity, public finances, and perhaps even its independence.

Both sides understood the importance of the campaigns in the north and thus deployed the bulk of their regulars along the border. There were four theaters of operation on the border, and their relative importance depended on how close they were to the centers of power, population, and commerce in the East. In ascending order of importance, these theaters were: (1) the

Old Northwest at the western end of Lake Erie, which was in play in 1812–13; (2) the Niagara front at the eastern end of the lake, a region that was fiercely contested throughout the war; (3) the St. Lawrence River, which was part of Britain's principal supply line to the West and which (unaccountably) the United States threatened only as part of its campaign against Montreal in 1813; and (4) the Lake Champlain-Richelieu River corridor, a traditional invasion route that the United States used to target Montreal in 1813 and the British when they marched to Plattsburgh in 1814.

The campaigns in these four theaters determined the outcome of the war, but there were five other theaters in North America as well as a sixth on the high seas. The other North American theaters were these: (1) the Old Southwest, where Jackson achieved his great victory over the Red Sticks; (2) the St. Louis Theater, where Americans skirmished with Britain's native allies throughout the war; (3) the coast of Maine, which the British occupied in 1814; (4) the Chesapeake Bay, which the British attacked in 1813 and 1814; and (5) the Gulf Coast, which the British threatened in 1814, after the end of the war in Europe had freed up troops on the Continent for service in North America.

A Polyglot Population in a Contested Region

The Gulf Coast in 1814 had a rich and diverse history and an uncertain future because it was contested ground that featured a polyglot population, shifting and uncertain government authority, and fluid boundaries. Spanish explorers claimed the region (which they called Florida) in the sixteenth century; missions and small settlements proliferated after St. Augustine was founded in 1565. At the time of European contact, Florida had a large native population—modern estimates suggest as many as 350,000—but these Indians were nearly wiped out by diseases brought by the explorers. This opened up lands for the Seminoles, an offshoot of the Creeks, who moved south into Florida in the late eighteenth century.

The Spanish population in Florida never exceeded 4,000, and as a weak and declining power, Spain's hold over its province was precarious. In the imperial wars of the seventeenth and eighteenth centuries, the Spanish had to fend off raids from the French and British. Because Florida was a haven for runaway slaves from South Carolina and Georgia, British settlers in those colonies were eager to conquer or at least neutralize it. Invasions from South

Carolina in 1702–4 took a particularly heavy toll on the Spanish missions and settlements.

In 1763, as part of the settlement at the end of the Seven Years War, Spain ceded Florida to Great Britain. Most of the Spanish population departed for Cuba, and for the next 20 years, the British ruled the province. To facilitate control, the British divided the territory into East Florida, extending from the Atlantic to the Apalachicola River (which includes modern Florida except for most of the panhandle), and West Florida, which extended from the Apalachicola to the Mississippi River (and today consists of the Florida panhandle and the southern portion of Alabama, Mississippi, and Louisiana). The British retained St. Augustine as the capital of East Florida and named Pensacola the capital of West Florida.

The British sought to attract settlers from South Carolina; a fair number responded, moving their plantations and slaves to East Florida. A sizeable number of indentured servants also emigrated to the province from southern Europe. In addition, the end of the Revolutionary War brought an influx of Loyalists from Georgia and South Carolina. British rule ended in 1784, when, as part of the settlement after the American Revolution, the Floridas were restored to Spain. Although the Spanish returned, many of the British planters remained. So, too, did British merchants, who now dominated trade in the region. They supplied needs not only of the settlers but also the Seminoles in northern Florida and the Lower Creeks in southern Georgia. The Spanish sanctioned some of the British commerce, but much trade was conducted illegally—by British and American merchants—in defiance of Spanish law.

Although the Spanish had recovered Florida, American independence meant that they now had to contend with a new and aggressive neighbor to the north. Especially threatening was Georgia, whose population jumped from 83,000 in 1790 to 252,000 by 1810. Although black slaves made up more than 40 percent of the population of Georgia, most of the whites were aggressively expansionistic and resented the fact that Spanish officials allowed Florida to become a sanctuary for runaway slaves and hostile Creeks and Seminoles. The Spanish in East Florida numbered only 3,700 in 1811, more than half of whom were free blacks or slaves. The only way that Spanish officials could counter the numerical superiority of their neighbors to the north was by arming blacks and employing native allies. The growing U.S. population in West Florida rendered the Spanish rule in that province even more precarious.

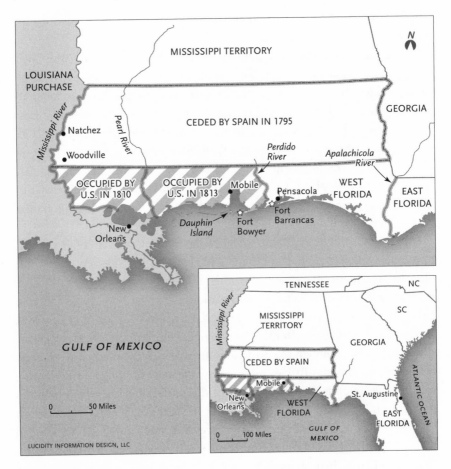

The Gulf Coast

American Inroads

The United States made steady inroads into the Gulf Coast at the expense of Spain. In the Pinckney Treaty of 1795, Spain agreed to permit Americans in the West to use the lower Mississippi (including the port city of New Orleans) to get their commodities to market. The Spanish also agreed to surrender their claims to nearly 6,000 square miles of land north of the 31st parallel. Eight years later, when the United States purchased Louisiana from France, Spanish Florida was left as an isolated and vulnerable European outpost on America's southern flank.

The United States occupied West Florida up to the Perdido River in stages between 1810 and 1813, claiming that it had been part of the Louisiana Purchase. The Spanish vigorously contested this dubious claim, but West Florida was virtually defenseless—with never more than 400 or 500 Spanish troops there to provide security—and with the American population in the western part of the province in open revolt, the Spanish had little choice but to withdraw to Pensacola when U.S. officials arrived to assume control.

In 1810–11 the U.S. government supported preparations for the occupation of East Florida, but an unauthorized invasion from Georgia in March 1812 met with resistance, and the result was a conflict known as the Patriot War. With war against Great Britain now on the horizon, the administration could see little advantage in waging a second war against Spanish Florida. Hence, it repudiated the invasion, although it sent U.S. troops to join the Georgia invaders in order to hold on to the Spanish territory they occupied. These troops were withdrawn a year later, but the Patriot War dragged on until the spring of 1814. The invaders robbed or killed residents who would not join them and burned their estates. Spanish officials countered by recruiting black troops and unleashing their Seminole allies, who waged their own vicious war against the invaders. As a result, virtually the entire countryside between the Georgia border and St. Augustine was devastated. The war ended when the last U.S. invaders withdrew. The conflict heightened distrust and exacerbated the already bitter feelings on the border.

Although at the end of the Patriot War East Florida remained in Spanish hands, Spain's hold over the province was as tenuous as ever. Local Spanish officials got their orders from Cuba, but no one in the Spanish new world could count on much guidance or aid from the mother country as long as the Napoleonic Wars continued. Spain was embroiled in those wars, both as a belligerent and, from 1808 on, as a major theater of operations. The Peninsular War in Europe (1808–1814), which included conventional campaigns and irregular warfare, consumed Spain and its resources and significantly weakened its hold over its territories in the New World.

The shifting imperial claims on the Gulf Coast left the region with what was probably the most diverse population in the New World. There were at least four nationalities present: the Spanish, French, British, and Americans. There were also numerous Seminoles and Creeks, and adding to the racial mix was a sizeable population of free blacks and slaves.

Cities on the Gulf Coast

By 1812 there were three significant port cities on the Gulf Coast: Pensacola (which remained in Spanish hands), Mobile (60 miles to the west, which the United States seized in 1813), and New Orleans (another 145 miles to the west, which the United States acquired in 1803 as part of the Louisiana Purchase). Pensacola (with no more than 1,000 people) and Mobile (with fewer than 500) were little more than villages but enjoyed a special status on the Gulf because of their commercial and strategic importance.

New Orleans, on the other hand, was the principal outlet for western produce and by the standards of the day a major U.S. city. With a population in 1810 of more than 17,000, it was the seventh largest city in the nation, and by 1814 the city and its suburbs exceeded 25,000. By a huge margin it was the dominant city in the West. Because the city was built on land that was virtually at sea level and was inundated with an average of 64 inches of rain a year, it was prone to flooding. Like most towns at the time, it was also subject to frequent fires. There was no readily available source of cobblestone, so the streets were mostly dirt; they were dusty in summer and muddy if not water-filled in winter.

The sidewalks, where they existed, were constructed mainly of wood that came from flatboats that brought cargoes down the river from the north but could not easily sail back upriver against the current and thus were broken up for their lumber. Open gutters in New Orleans were supposed to carry rainwater, raw sewage from humans and animals, and other debris away from the main streets, but in the rainy season gutters and streets sometimes did not drain for days or weeks at a time. The entire river delta was a breeding ground for tropical diseases (particularly yellow fever) that took a heavy toll on the human population. Brigadier General James Wilkinson lost half of his command to disease and desertion within a year of making camp in 1809 at Terre aux Boeufs, a particularly unhealthy spot southeast of New Orleans.

The population of New Orleans included people of French and Spanish descent, a growing number of Americans, and a smattering of British subjects and people from other parts of Europe. The racial mix was also diverse. The census of 1810 showed about an equal number of whites, free people of color (mostly mulattos but some blacks, Indians, and mestizos), and slaves (mostly blacks but with some mulattos and mestizos). Almost half of the entire population of the city consisted of refugees from Haiti, most of whom had arrived in a huge migration that took place in 1809–10 when they were evicted from Spanish-controlled Cuba. They had been granted sanctuary in Cuba when they fled from war-torn Haiti in 1803, but that status was revoked when Spain broke with Napoleonic France in 1808. The refugee population served to reinforce the French character of New Orleans, and it was not until the 1830s that English replaced French as the most common language.

New Orleans was a typical borderlands city in that liquor flowed freely, prostitution and gambling flourished, and violence was commonplace. But in a host of ways the city was unique. It had a rich French, Spanish, and Catholic heritage, and the law, social mores, and architecture reflected that legacy. Unlike other U.S. cities, in which Sunday was a day of rest, in New Orleans it was devoted to shopping, parties, balls, and other amusements. The Crescent City also differed from the rest of the slave belt in that it was comparatively easy for slaves to buy their freedom. Free people of color enjoyed more rights and even had their own militia companies. When Rachel Jackson visited the city with her husband in 1821, she described her impressions to a friend: "It reminds me," she said, "of those words in Revelations: 'Great Babylon is come up before me.' Oh, the wickedness, the idolatry of this place! Unspeakable the riches and splendor."[1]

Because it was a major commercial port, people and money flowed freely into and out of the city in normal times, but with the nation at war, the presence of British warships in the Gulf had curtailed much of that movement. Cotton and sugar were the two principal cash crops in the region, but without any way to safely ship these commodities to other parts of the United States or abroad, prices steadily declined. This worked a hardship on everyone, but as a wide-open city New Orleans offered other opportunities to make money.

There was a large renegade population of seamen known as the Baratarian pirates living in the delta who made their living preying on merchant vessels in the Gulf. Led by Jean and Pierre Lafitte, the Baratarians numbered around 1,000 at peak, but their numbers had declined significantly by 1814. They sailed under dubious privateering commissions issued mainly by the South American city of Cartagena, which had declared independence from Spain in 1811. Although authorized to cruise against Spanish commerce, they sometimes seized ships flying other flags, which suggests that they were more akin to pirates.

Even though the Baratarians operated beyond the law, they traded freely with New Orleans, buoying the city's economy. City and state officials were nearly powerless to halt the steady flow of booty into New Orleans in defiance of U.S. tax and trade laws and in violation of U.S. sovereignty. There were armed confrontations between the pirates and federal customs officials, and in late November 1814 when the governor offered a $500 reward for Jean Lafitte's capture, the Baratarian leader countered by offering a $1,000 reward for the capture of the governor.

A Gulf Coast Campaign

The Gulf Coast offered an inviting theater of operations for the British in the War of 1812. The region was readily accessible to the Royal Navy and yet remote and inaccessible to the United States. With the British in control of the high seas, the Gulf Coast could be supplied only by flatboats or barges from Pennsylvania, Kentucky, and Tennessee that floated down western rivers to the Mississippi River and then to New Orleans. Under the best of circumstances—with no stops, storms, or snags—this trip took weeks. From Pittsburgh the typical flatboat took six or seven weeks to reach New Orleans. Steamships cut the transit time dramatically, but they were just now making an appearance on American waters.

Much of the war material needed for military operations in the West had to be shipped across the Appalachian Mountains—typically from Philadelphia to Pittsburgh—always a costly and time-consuming process. There were western cities with small and growing manufacturing establishments, most notably Pittsburgh (with 4,800 people in 1810), Lexington (with 4,300), and Cincinnati (with 2,500), but they could not begin to supply the needs of the war effort on the Canadian frontier, let alone in the Southwest and on the Gulf Coast. The recurring supply problems that Andrew Jackson faced in the Creek War were far from unique and illustrated the extraordinary logistical challenges of waging war in the West.

The political and ethnic loyalties of people on the Gulf Coast also made it an attractive target for the British. Spain was in control of East Florida and after 1807 was allied to Great Britain. Although eager to avoid being drawn into the War of 1812 and suspicious of any British operations on the Gulf Coast, Spanish officials had no one else to turn to when the United States threatened. Moreover, the Spanish, British, and Seminole people in Florida had little love for the United States, and the French and Spanish in Louisiana had never become fully reconciled to U.S. rule. The slave population on the Gulf Coast might also welcome a British invasion, much as it had in the Chesapeake. In short, the British recognized that they might receive a friendly reception from many residents if they invaded.

As early as 1812, Sir John Borlase Warren, who had command of the Royal Navy on the American station, recommended a descent onto the Gulf Coast to draw American troops off from Canada. Charles Cameron, the Royal governor of the Bahamas in Nassau, also recommended attacking the Gulf Coast. Nassau was on the edge of the Caribbean Basin, and British merchants regularly supplied Cameron with intelligence from the region that he passed on to London. The merchants reported that the Indians preferred British manufactured goods and would welcome a British presence on the Gulf. They also brought back tales of discontent with American rule among the French and Spanish in Louisiana and suggested that the defenses of New Orleans were so weak that the city would be easy to capture.

Governor Cameron received letters from the Lower Creeks and Seminoles inviting an alliance against the United States. Although these Indians were not at war with the young republic, they feared that they soon would be and that their lands would be taken from them. They had strong commercial ties to the British and had long enjoyed friendly relations with them. Hence, they were likely to make good allies. Cameron forwarded these letters along with other intelligence from the Gulf Coast to his superiors in London.

The reports emanating from the Caribbean piqued British interest in the Gulf Coast, although London officials were reluctant to commit the large force that they thought would be needed to make the campaign a success. But in the summer of 1814 Vice Admiral Sir Alexander Cochrane, who had replaced Admiral Warren on the American station the previous April, threw his support behind the campaign and suggested far fewer British troops would be needed to make it a success.

In May Cochrane had dispatched Captain Hugh Pigot with a shipload of arms for the natives on the Apalachicola River in East Florida. Pigot was accompanied by George Woodbine, a well-regarded young Jamaican who had traded with the Indians and thus knew them. Woodbine was given a lieutenant's commission in the Royal Marines and ordered to distribute the arms. Although the Seminoles and Creeks on the Gulf were interested in the British initiative, they were desperately short of not only arms but also food and clothing. Woodbine did not have the resources to meet their needs. Moreover, they were relentlessly harassed by raiding parties that Jackson sent south in the wake of his victory at Horseshoe Bend.

Based on Pigot's report on the mission, Cochrane told his superiors that a Gulf Coast campaign could succeed with as few as 3,000 troops. His plan was to step up raids on the Atlantic coast as a diversion, seize Mobile, and use it as a base for operations first against U.S. forts on the Alabama River and then against New Orleans. The seizure of Mobile, he thought, would draw a large number of natives to the British standard. Cochrane also planned to recruit runaway slaves, much as he had in the Chesapeake. If disaffected Spanish and French residents in Louisiana and the Baratarian pirates also flocked to the British standard, the campaign was even more likely to succeed.

Cochrane's plan suggested that with a modest investment of men and material the British could open up another major front in the War of 1812. This would force the United States to redeploy its scarce resources to a new theater of operations that it would find difficult, if not impossible, to adequately supply. British leaders endorsed Cochrane's plan and put the admiral in charge of the fleet that would carry out the operation. Major General Robert Ross, the hero of the occupation of Washington, was charged with heading the expedition on land. He would enjoy the support of two first-class staff officers, Alexander Dickson, who was considered the best artillery officer in the British army, and John Fox Burgoyne, an experienced engineer who was the illegitimate son of Major General John Burgoyne, the man responsible for the British defeat at Saratoga in 1777.

By the time that officials in London had approved of Cochrane's plan, circumstances on both sides of the Atlantic had changed dramatically. The Red Sticks had been defeated in the Creek War in the spring of 1814, which significantly limited the contribution they were likely to make to the campaign. The war in Europe also had ended, which freed up thousands of British veterans for service in America. The British could now conduct a major campaign on the Gulf Coast without local assistance. Moreover, with Anglo-American peace talks on the horizon, the objective of the campaign changed. Instead of trying to take the pressure off Canada, British leaders now sought to secure territory that they could use as a bargaining chip in the peace negotiations.

The British government instructed Ross "to obtain a Command of the Embouchure [mouth] of the Mississippi, so as to deprive the back Settlements of America of their Communication with the sea" and "to occupy some important & valuable possession, by the restoration of which we may improve the Conditions of Peace, or which may entitle us to exact its Cession as the price of Peace." Ross was to encourage the free inhabitants to revolt but was to make no binding promises about their future. "You must give them clearly to understand that Great Britain cannot pledge herself to make the Independence of Louisiana, or its restoration to the Spanish Crown, a *sine qua non* [an essential requirement] of Peace with the United States."[2]

Pensacola and Mobile

In accordance with his plan, Cochrane in August 1814 sent another small British force under Major Edward Nicolls of the Royal Marines to the Apalachicola. Nicolls was in the middle of a long and distinguished military career that would span nearly 40 years and that would involve so many actions that he was wounded numerous times. At Apalachicola, he was to distribute more arms, raise a force of natives and blacks, and scout the area as a prelude to major operations. After landing his arms and as much food as he could spare, Nicolls sailed to Pensacola, arriving on August 14. When the Spanish asked for his cooperation to repel an expected U.S. attack, Nicolls occupied the two forts that commanded the entrance to the harbor and assumed command over the entire city.

To maintain his position in Pensacola, Nicolls ordered the remaining British troops on the Apalachicola to join him. He also recruited Indians as well as virtually the entire slave population in Pensacola. The fresh recruits started looting Pensacola and in other ways menaced local residents. The loss of their slave property coupled with the looting alienated the Spanish population. Nicolls responded by tightening his hold on the city.

Andrew Jackson was not surprised by the arrival of the British on the Gulf Coast. Along with other westerners, he believed (erroneously) that British agents were working with the Red Sticks and fully expected the British to attack the Gulf Coast. By the summer of 1814 newspaper stories in the Caribbean seemed to confirm his suspicions. With the Admiralty buying provisions and boats in the West Indies, a campaign against the Gulf Coast seemed likely. Moreover, with the war in Europe now over, the British were sending transports with troops to America, and it was widely believed that their destination was the Gulf Coast.

Ever alert to good intelligence, Jackson received confidential information from Vincent Gray, an American merchant in the West Indies, that confirmed these reports. According to Gray, Major Nicolls boasted that he would make quick work of the United States because it was populated by a "cowardly and dastardly set who knew nothing of warfare and when their own slaves were turned upon them would soon flee the country."[3] Gray sent similar reports to officials in Washington and Louisiana.

Jackson's network of native and American spies alerted him when the British made their first appearance on the Apalachicola in May. One even procured a musket that had been distributed by George Woodbine to the Indians there. Later on, Jackson's spies informed him when the British took control of Pensacola. Like the British, he considered Pensacola, with its superb harbor, the key to the campaign. "Pensacola," he said, "is more important to the British arms than any other point on our South or Southwest."[4] Jackson had tasked one spy with reporting on the defenses of Pensacola, so he had an excellent description if, as seemed likely, he decided to move against the city. News that the British were lining up Indian allies and recruiting slaves only added to his determination to act.

Having arrived in Mobile on August 22 with a little more than 500 regulars, Jackson made the city his command center. The United States had taken Mobile from the Spanish the previous year. The port was protected by a dilapidated post named Fort Bowyer, which was located at the end of a peninsula that commanded the entrance to Mobile Bay, 30 miles south of Mobile. Capture of this post would isolate the city and make it vulnerable to a naval attack. Jackson strengthened Fort Bowyer and garrisoned it with 160 seasoned troops under Major William Lawrence. Although the fort remained vulnerable, at least now it could offer some resistance to an attack.

The British struck on September 12, landing 225 Royal Marines and Indians under Major Nicolls on the coast near Fort Bowyer. Marching to the post, the British (who carried one howitzer) exchanged some artillery fire with the Americans but waited for their naval support to arrive before launching an attack. On September 15, a British naval squadron headed by HMS *Hermes* (22 guns), Captain William H. Percy commanding, commenced a bombardment. But the water was too shallow for the British ships, and the *Hermes* ran aground within range of the American guns, forcing Percy to abandon the ship and order it destroyed. Nicolls launched a simultaneous attack by land, but without naval support, he had little choice but to abandon it and return to Pensacola.

When Jackson, who was in Mobile, learned that Fort Bowyer was under attack, he sent reinforcements. But the men could not get near the fort as long as it was under bombardment. When they saw an explosion, they assumed it was the fort, rather than the British ship, that been destroyed and returned to Mobile with the news the fort had fallen. Jackson was skeptical but prepared to retake it when news arrived from Major Lawrence of the U.S. victory. Fort Bowyer—and thus Mobile—remained in American hands. The British had sustained about 70 casualties compared to around 20 for the United States.

Jackson's Response

Having rebuffed the British at Mobile, Jackson was eager to move against Pensacola. He had exchanged several letters with the Spanish governor at Pensacola in which the hot-tempered Tennessean had been insulting, belligerent, and provocative, breathing fire with almost every word. He accused the Spanish of conniving with the British against the United States and, even more infuriating, of arming and protecting the Red Sticks, whom he characterized as "a murderous rebellious barbarous Banditti who have not only imbrued [stained] their hands in the innocent blood of our helpless women and children, but raised the exterminating Hatchet against their own nation."[5]

Calling Pensacola "the Hotbed of the war and the asylum of our enemies," Jackson had asked the administration for permission to seize the Spanish city, but officials in Washington were unwilling to sanction any action that might draw Spain into the war.[6] In October 1814 the secretary of war ordered Jackson to steer clear of Spanish territory, but for some reason this order did not reach the general until long after he had acted.

By late September the administration had received intelligence that the British planned to attack Louisiana and ordered the governor of Tennessee to send 5,000 militia or volunteers to Jackson. Similar orders asked Kentucky for 2,500 men. In the wake of Jackson's success in the Creek War, the response was enthusiastic. Still, it was a month before Jackson had the troops he needed to act. In the meantime he was frequently immobilized by recurring bouts of dysentery. Visitors were surprised at how worn and haggard he looked.

By the end of October Jackson had amassed over 4,000 regulars, volunteers, and Choctaw and Chickasaw Indians and was ready to attack Pensacola. Since he was acting without orders, he sent Secretary of War James Monroe a letter justifying his decision to seize the Spanish city. He argued that the expedition was necessary for "the safety of this section of the Union" because the British and Indians were using Pensacola as a base of operations against the United States.[7]

On October 29 Jackson departed from Mobile with 3,000 men, reaching the outskirts of the Spanish city a week later. By this time the British had thoroughly worn out their welcome in Pensacola. The Spanish governor of West Florida, who had only about 500 troops at his disposal, was unsure whether to offer resistance to Jackson's force. Jackson decoyed the Spanish into thinking that he planned to attack from the west, although he moved most of his troops around the city to the east. From this direction, he was able to march into Pensacola on November 7 without meeting much resistance. There was some skirmishing, with 15 or 20 casualties on each side, but then the Spanish governor surrendered, and Jackson took control of the city.

Disgusted with the lack of Spanish backbone, the British blew up the two harbor forts and withdrew to Apalachicola. They took with them not only their slave recruits but also 200 Spanish soldiers (mostly black recruits from Cuba), who were forced to perform labor on the Apalachicola for the remainder of the war. In contrast to the British, Jackson treated his prize with respect, and there was no looting. He even ordered the return of a Spanish flag and some church artifacts taken when his army departed. His scrupulous behavior endeared him to Spanish officials.

With the harbor forts destroyed, Pensacola was now defenseless, and Jackson could not hold the city against a seaborne attack. Even so, he had driven out the British and disrupted their plans for recruiting additional Indian allies and runaway slaves. Jackson, who still expected the British to seize Mobile before attacking New Orleans, abandoned Pensacola on November 9 and ten days later reached Mobile.

Jackson sent a report to Monroe shortly after the operation, and upon returning to Mobile he followed up with another letter that showed his growing penchant, especially in the wake of his successes in the field, for lecturing his superiors. "Let me state," he said, "that it is with nations as with individuals: let them sternly know that our rights will be respected, that the least infringement will be punished, and they will respect your rights and live in good neighborhood."[8]

Jackson dispatched 1,000 regulars to harass the Indians north of Apalachicola and another 2,000 troops under Brigadier General John Coffee to Baton Rouge, where he could rendezvous with additional troops coming in from Tennessee and be well positioned to march to either Mobile or New

Orleans. Jackson also strengthened Fort Bowyer and increased the number of troops assigned to Mobile. To command these troops, he chose Brigadier General James Winchester, who had surrendered at Frenchtown in early 1813 but had since joined his fellow Tennessean on the Gulf. Finally realizing that the British were likely to attack New Orleans directly, Jackson left Mobile with his staff on November 22, reaching the Crescent City on the morning of December 1. Despite constant rain and high waters, he made decent time, averaging sixteen miles a day. The trip enabled him to study approaches to the Crescent City from the east.

By the time that Jackson had left Mobile, a large British force of about 5,500 troops plus personnel from the Royal Navy and Marines had assembled in Jamaica for a major campaign on the Gulf Coast. Several thousand additional troops were en route from Europe. Since Mobile was still in U.S. hands, Admiral Cochrane decided to sail for New Orleans and attack the city directly from below. Because Major General Robert Ross had been killed outside of Baltimore in September 1814, the British government assigned his command to Major General Edward Pakenham.

On November 28, 1814, while Pakenham was still in transit across the Atlantic, Cochrane departed from Jamaica on his 80-gun flagship, H.M.S. *Tonnant*. He led a fleet of 50 ships, ranging from ships-of-the-line to schooners and including nearly a dozen transports. The armada arrived off the coast of Florida on December 5. An attempt to recruit natives failed, although given the size of their force the British hardly needed native help for the campaign. On December 13, Cochrane's armada arrived at Cat Island, about 85 miles northeast of New Orleans and thus within striking distance.

New Orleans Vulnerable

Long before Cochrane's armada arrived on the Gulf Coast, the British had laid the groundwork for an attack on New Orleans. The previous August Major Edward Nicolls tried to line up local support by issuing a bombastic proclamation calling on the French and Spanish in Louisiana "to assist in liberating from a faithless and imbecile government your paternal soil."[9] When Jackson got a copy of Nicolls's proclamation, he responded with a pair of proclamations of his own.

Jackson's first proclamation appealed to everyone in Louisiana to come to the defense of New Orleans. Jackson made a special appeal to the large

French population, reminding all that the British were "the natural and sworn enemies of all Frenchmen" and expressing confidence "that every Louisianan, either by birth or adoption, will promptly obey the voice of his country; will rally round the eagle of Columbia, secure it from the pending danger, or nobly die in the last ditch in its defense." Anyone who refused, he added ominously, "deserves to be a slave, and must be punished as an enemy to his country, and a friend to her foe."[10] Jackson's second proclamation urged free blacks in Louisiana to enlist in the U.S. Army. "As a distinct, independent battalion or regiment, pursuing the path of glory," he promised, "you will, undivided, receive the applause and gratitude of your countrymen."[11]

The local population was unmoved by Jackson's appeal and little inclined to offer any resistance to a British invasion. Even though the United States had acquired Louisiana more than a decade before, and Louisiana was admitted to the Union in 1812, few of the French or Spanish residents were happy with either the new order or with the state of war that now existed with Great Britain. With British warships patrolling the Gulf and Caribbean, the export of American commodities had plummeted. By the end of 1814 the city's warehouses were filled with 150,000 bales of cotton, 10,000 hogsheads of sugar, and huge quantities of other commodities that had been floated down the Mississippi. A local merchant put the total value of all the warehoused goods at a staggering $20 million.

A good deal of tension existed among different groups in this heterogeneous population, tension that on occasion erupted in violence, particularly between the Creoles (those born in New Orleans, especially the French) and the recent American immigrants (who constituted less than 15 percent of the population). Much of the population in New Orleans radiated apathy, if not disloyalty. "The War of the U.S. is very unpopular with us," reported John Windship, a transplanted New Englander, in early 1814. French and Spanish residents were called up for militia duty but "absolutely refused to be marched" and "declared themselves liege [loyal] subjects of Spain and France." If the British attacked, Windship concluded, "there is no force competent to repel them."[12]

Before 1814 no one had expected New Orleans to be targeted, and thus little had been done to prepare its defenses. The local commanders had done nothing and had thoroughly alienated the city's population. Brigadier General James Wilkinson, who was in charge until 1813, had squandered the resources at his disposal and feuded with navy personnel assigned to the station.

By 1813 Wilkinson had so angered local residents that Louisiana's two Democratic-Republican U.S. senators threatened to join the opposition in Congress if he were not removed. The administration had responded by ordering him to the St. Lawrence River front, where he had taken part in the ill-fated double-barreled operation against Montreal. His successor, Major General Thomas Flournoy, openly distrusted the French and Spanish residents and had no faith in the local militia. This did not endear him to the city's residents. "*Few, very few,*" he complained in March 1814, "are disposed to aid the General Government in the present crisis."[13]

William C. C. Claiborne, a native of Virginia and the brother of General Ferdinand Claiborne, had been the territorial governor and was easily elected as the state's first governor in 1812, but he took a lofty view of his power and privileges and feuded with the state legislature, particularly a band of French Creoles who controlled the senate. In fact, in early 1814, when the governor threatened to prosecute those who failed to show for militia duty, some talked of impeaching him. Claiborne also clashed with some of the American immigrants, most notably Edward Livingston, an influential lawyer who was a scion of one of the most powerful families in New York. As a result of his feuds, Claiborne was unable to muster much support for defense measures until the British were practically on the coast.

The Louisiana militia could not be counted on to stop a British invasion. Although there were a number of uniformed local militia units who were ready to serve, they had no interest in performing the labor needed to prepare defensive works. It was also unclear how dependable they would be in the heat of battle. The rest of the militia units were untrained, poorly armed, and—especially in New Orleans—ill-disposed to turn out when summoned. Militia who turned out from the interior bitterly resented the failure of city militia to do their duty and responded by deserting in large numbers. On one day alone, 40 citizen soldiers went home. Fearing that the rest would soon follow suit, Claiborne dismissed them all.

Claiborne had lived in Tennessee from 1794 to 1801 and knew Jackson. Throughout the late summer of 1814 he peppered the Tennessee general with letters warning that the city's population would not come to its defense. He also expressed fear of a slave revolt. The British occupation of Pensacola in August exacerbated local fears. With the enemy "in possession of Pensacola," said a correspondent from New Orleans in September, "this country is in a state of great alarm."[14]

Compounding these ills, there was a cash shortage in New Orleans. The local banks (like most other banks in the nation) were insolvent and unwilling to make loans. Only reluctantly did they agree in November to lend Claiborne $20,000 to finance some defense measures. The legislature approved of this loan and later appropriated an additional $11,000, but the money was pointedly appropriated for Jackson's use rather than the governor's.

Little wonder that before Jackson's arrival there was widespread talk in New Orleans of preserving the city by surrendering it. Among those urging this action were some longtime British residents. Surrender was not unprecedented in this war. When threatened by a British squadron the previous August, the Federalist city of Alexandria, Virginia, had surrendered, and the British had sailed down the Potomac to the Chesapeake with 21 prize ships filled with flour, tobacco, cotton, sugar, and other commodities. Republican newspapers denounced Alexandria for not putting up a fight, but the city had escaped destruction, and its surrender was not unique.

Many towns on Cape Cod paid tribute to avoid bombardment and plundering. The Republican-dominated island of Nantucket declared its neutrality in the war so that it could trade with the mainland and resume its fishing. Similarly, the federal government cut off all trade with Block Island (which was part of Rhode Island) because it was cooperating with a nearby British fleet.

Jackson Takes Charge

When Jackson rode into New Orleans on December 1, he was greeted by the governor, mayor, Master Commandant Daniel T. Patterson (the ranking U.S. Navy officer), Edward Livingston, and other community leaders. Jackson, now 47 and with steel gray hair, still had his erect military bearing, but a year of hard campaigning coupled with the ravages of dysentery and perhaps malaria and his still-festering shoulder wound (from the Benton brawl) had left him gaunt and ghostlike with a sickly yellow complexion. Those who welcomed him were surprised by his appearance, but his record of success in the Creek War was undeniable. After the governor read a welcoming address, Jackson responded and then moved into a brick building that served as his headquarters.

Jackson next turned his attention to the defense of the city. Ever since coming to the Gulf Coast he had received reports about how exposed New

Orleans was. Several months earlier he had ordered the regulars assigned to the station to beef up the river defenses, but the city was still vulnerable. Fortunately for the United States, it was not an easy target. Unlike most port cities on the Atlantic Coast, the Crescent City was nearly 100 miles up the Mississippi River. This made it difficult for an enemy to approach from any direction.

The city could not easily be attacked from the west. There was ready access to Barataria Bay, which was 70 miles southwest of New Orleans, but between the bay and the Mississippi River there was nothing but a confusing maze of narrow and shallow waterways surrounded by a huge swamp. Nor could the city be easily attacked by sailing up the river. The strong current and a bar at the mouth prevented large warships from venturing up the river, and smaller ships had to contend with two fortifications on the river—Fort St. Philip, which was 30 miles from the mouth, and Fort St. Leon, which was another 60 miles upriver, just 10 miles south of New Orleans. Both forts would have to be reduced by an enemy using the river approach, and the British assault on Fort McHenry the previous summer had shown how difficult it was to compel a well-built fort to submit even when bomb and rocket ships were used. Moreover, Fort St. Leon was located on a bend in the river known as the English Turn, where sailing ships often had to wait for the wind to shift before they could move through an S-shaped turn. In the meantime, they were sitting ducks.

New Orleans could best be approached from the East, but here, too, an invading force was likely to encounter tough going to get through the swamps and bayous to reach the city. The biggest advantage that an invader enjoyed was the many avenues of approach. From Cat Island, where the British landed, they could attack from at least three directions: from the east via Lake Borgne, from the north via Lake Pontchartrain, or from the northeast via the landmass between the lakes, which was known as the Plain of Gentilly. And if the British approached via one of the lakes, there were any number of landing sites they could use. This meant Jackson needed a good intelligence system to give adequate warning of the route taken by the enemy.

Jackson lost no time in preparing for the coming storm. His energy, confidence, and resolve had a remarkable impact on the local population. "General Jackson," wrote one contemporary, "electrified all hearts." "His immediate and incessant attention to the defense of the country," said another, "soon convinced all that he was the man the occasion demanded."[15] The defeatism that earlier had been so evident disappeared, and talk of surrendering to the British ended. Instead, as one witness put it, "The streets resounded with *Yankee Doodle*, the *Marseilles Hymn*, the *Chant du Depart*, and other martial airs."[16]

Jackson accepted Edward Livingston as his unofficial aide and confidential adviser. This was a good choice. Livingston knew French, understood local law, and was a good stylist. Although he was an enemy of Governor Claiborne, Livingston put aside all differences. As head of the Citizens' Committee of Defense, he made the safety of New Orleans his top priority. Jackson and Livingston had met in Washington in the 1790s and had been friends ever since, but it was their close collaboration in New Orleans that marked the beginning of an especially fruitful relationship that persisted for the rest of their lives.

Jackson's next order of business was to master the local geography. He relied heavily on his own engineer, Major Howell Tatum, and even more on 36-year-old Arsène Lacarrière Latour, a local architect and engineer, who was taken into the army with the rank of major. Latour had earlier prepared detailed maps of the area, and Jackson found his advice indispensable. Jackson spent a week touring the area with Latour and Tatum. He ordered all water approaches to the city blocked with felled trees and batteries established at key points. Although Jackson did not enjoy the unparalleled intelligence that his American and native spies provided in the Creek War and in Spanish Florida, he nonetheless set up a good network that would keep him abreast of enemy movements.

What Jackson needed most to meet the huge British army that was known to be en route was troops. Governor Claiborne called out some militia, and (in sharp contrast to the response earlier in the year) a fair number of men showed up for duty. General John Coffee remained in Baton Rouge with his mounted volunteers. Jackson was as yet unwilling to commit these troops to New Orleans. Jackson earlier had appealed to members of the large free black community in New Orleans to enlist in the regular army. Jackson also accepted into service two battalions of free black militia. One battalion, 280 strong, was local; the second, 150 men, consisted mostly of refugees from Haiti under the command of Captain Joseph Savary. Some whites in New Orleans objected, but Jackson brushed their objections aside. Even so, by mid-December, Jackson had only about 2,000 troops at New Orleans.

The Battle of Lake Borgne. British forces overcame a formidable array of American gunboats with many smaller craft that carried more firepower. The defeat alarmed Jackson and New Orleans residents. (Painting by Thomas L. Hornbrook. The Historical New Orleans Collection, Acc. No. 1950.54)

The Battle of Lake Borgne (December 14, 1814)

The U.S. Navy at New Orleans also faced a manpower shortage. Daniel T. Patterson's squadron consisted of the U.S. Sloop *Louisiana* (22 guns), the U.S. Schooner *Carolina* (16 guns), and six gunboats. The *Carolina* arrived from Charleston with a full crew, and Patterson's gunboats were manned, but the *Louisiana* was a converted merchantman without a crew. Patterson tried to recruit local seamen but without success. Most tars shunned the service because they viewed the navy as an enemy of the illegal trade in the Gulf that was the source of many jobs. The navy's destruction of the Baratarian base on Grand Terre Island on September 16, 1814, had further alienated the seafaring population.

Patterson sent five of his gunboats with 23 guns, manned by 185 men under Lieutenant Thomas ap Catesby Jones, to the eastern end of Lake Borgne to keep an eye out for the British. The British spotted Jones's boats, and Cochrane sent 42 small barges with 43 guns, manned by 1,200 men under the command of Captain Nicholas Lockyer, to capture the American flotilla. Rather than engage in a battle, Jones had orders to withdraw to a fort called Petites Coquilles at the Rigolets, which was the strait that connected Lake Pontchartrain to Lake Borgne. But with the wind blowing toward the Gulf, the water level dropped, and some of Jones's boats ran aground.

Jones managed to free his boats, but then the loss of wind coupled with the force of the ebb tide prevented him from reaching Petites Coquilles. On December 14, he prepared to engage the approaching British barges, which had reached the American flotilla the previous day after 36 hours of arduous rowing. Outmanned and outgunned, the U.S. flotilla gave a good account of itself but was overwhelmed and had to surrender. In the Battle of Lake Borgne, the Americans sustained about 40 casualties, including Jones, the British about 100, including Lockyer. The United States also lost the *Sea Horse,* a dispatch boat that was filled with naval stores for New Orleans. Unable to escape the British, Sailing Master William Johnson blew up the boat and its stores. The United States could ill afford to lose any of these boats, and Jackson was now without any eyes on Lake Borgne.

5   A Glorious Victory

NEWS OF the Battle of Lake Borgne sent shock waves through New Orleans and the rest of Louisiana. It revealed that the British had arrived and meant business. Jackson responded by ordering troops stationed elsewhere in the region to converge on New Orleans. General Coffee raced 850 mounted Tennessee volunteers from Baton Rouge, covering 135 miles in three days. His men made camp just five miles north of the city. Major Thomas Hinds brought 150 additional mounted regulars from Woodville, Mississippi, covering 230 miles in four days, and Major General William Carroll arrived shortly after via flatboat with 2,000 volunteer militia from Tennessee. The arrival of these troops raised Jackson's strength to more than 5,000 men. To provide still more manpower, Governor Claiborne issued *levée en masse*, which called all remaining militia into service.

The Louisiana legislature also responded to the crisis. It suspended debt collection and closed the courts to all civil suits for four months. It also appropriated $6,000 for bounties to encourage seamen to enlist in the navy and required all seamen to register for possible naval service, in effect sanctioning impressment. In addition, all merchant vessels were embargoed in port so that seamen would have no other employment opportunities. This

combination of laws coupled with bounties offered by Patterson finally secured enough seamen to man the *Louisiana.*

Martial Law

Jackson called on the legislature to suspend the right of habeas corpus
so that he could impress men into service and jail anyone who refused to
cooperate. But the legislature, no doubt mindful of the military despotism
of Brigadier General James Wilkinson in New Orleans during the Burr Conspiracy in 1806, was reluctant to suspend so basic a right. A committee asked
federal judge Dominick Hall for his opinion, and he replied that the Constitution authorized Congress alone to take this action. Hence, the legislature
refused to act.

Jackson responded on December 16 by taking matters into his own hands,
proclaiming martial law, and giving himself unprecedented control over the
city, which he now treated as a military camp subject to military rules. Not
only could he impress men into service, but he could regulate the movement
of people and information into and out of New Orleans. Jackson's decision
met with little opposition and in fact was approved by most local officials.
Only later, when Jackson was slow to lift martial law and jailed those who
objected, did it generate a firestorm of controversy that ultimately landed
Old Hickory in a court of law.

Jackson also issued a proclamation to dispel the "seditious reports" propagated by "British emissaries" that Britain planned to conquer Louisiana to
restore it to Spain. He called on everyone to defend the land from invasion,
and in typical Jacksonian fashion he hinted at the fate of those who shirked
their duty. "Those who are not for us," he said, "are against us, and will be
dealt with accordingly."[1]

The Baratarian Pirates

The Baratarian pirates offered another possible source of manpower. The
British had sent a special mission to their base on Grand Terre Island in September to entice them to join the invaders. The pirates were well armed and
knew how to use their weapons, and their knowledge of the river delta was
unmatched. The British offered Jean Lafitte a commission in their armed
services (probably in the Colonial Marines) and promised that Lafitte and

his men would receive land in America once the campaign was over. Lafitte stalled for time, telling the British that he needed two weeks to dispose of Britain's enemies in his camp and to put his affairs in order. But instead he immediately sent the documents the British had given him to Governor Claiborne and offered to join the American cause.

Even though the U.S. Navy destroyed his base shortly after the British visit, Lafitte was still willing to help defend New Orleans. As a Frenchman, he had no love for the British, and he believed that siding with the United States would best serve his interests. The pirates had promised Edward Livingston $20,000 if he could secure their acquittal of charges that they violated American trade laws. Livingston advised Lafitte that the best way to achieve this goal was to enlist under the American banner. It also offered the best chance of recovering a huge quantity of property that the United States had seized from the pirates when their base was destroyed.

When Jackson learned of the British offer, he publicly characterized the pirates as "hellish Banditti."[2] And even when he learned that Lafitte and his men had offered to join his cause, he refused to consider it. After the Battle of Lake Borgne, however, a local committee lobbied Jackson to change his mind. At the same time the legislature adopted a resolution to suspend legal proceedings against any Baratarian who enlisted in U.S. service. Governor Claiborne followed up with a proclamation to the same effect. Judge Hall added his support by ordering the release of any jailed Baratarian who agreed to serve.

Judge Hall also issued a pass to Jean Lafitte to enter the city. Lafitte visited Jackson on December 18, and his appeal, which had the support of nearly everyone in the city, worked. Jackson finally relented because he realized that the Baratarians' knowledge of the local geography and their fighting skills, especially as artillerymen, would make them useful allies. Lafitte got on so well with Jackson that he became Old Hickory's unofficial aide-de-camp, delivering messages and performing other staff duties for the commanding general.

About 50 Baratarians joined the American cause and performed good service manning one of Jackson's eight artillery batteries during the main battle. Afterwards, the Louisiana legislature asked Madison to pardon them, which he did. But Lafitte never recovered the property that had been seized. Later he resumed his privateering career and served as a spy for the Spanish. This had no impact on the inflated reputation that he enjoyed forever after in the public memory for his role in the defense of New Orleans. In fact, the National Park Service has designated the six sites in the New Orleans area that include the battlefield the Jean Lafitte National Historical Park and Preserve.

Jackson now had about 7,000 regulars, militia, and volunteers at his disposal. He assigned the militia and local volunteers to guard approaches or man forts, while keeping his best troops in New Orleans, ready to strike when he learned of the British approach. He was confident that the British could get nowhere near the city without his knowledge. Events were to prove otherwise.

The Night Attack (December 23, 1814)

Having disposed of the U.S gunboats, the British spent almost a week moving their base from Cat Island to Pea Island, which was located at the mouth of the Pearl River just 30 miles east of New Orleans. The ten-hour trip was made in open boats, and constant rainfall drenched the men en route. There was no relief when they reached Pea Island because it was barren and swampy; temperatures plummeted and the wind picked up. Although primitive shanties were erected for some of the officers, the men were stuck in the open without tents. With no firewood available, everyone suffered. Provisions had to be ferried in from the fleet and were limited to naval rations.

Rear Admiral Edward Codrington reported that the morning of December 19 "produced a N.-W. gale as bitter cold as we could have felt in England; and the nights of the 19th and 20th were so severe as to produce ice an inch thick in [water] tubs." The cold weather did not let up for a week. "Neither day nor night," lamented Codrington, "can we contrive to make ourselves comfortably warm."[3] The weather worked a particular hardship on black troops recruited in the West Indies, most of whom had never experienced these temperatures and wore lightweight clothing. A number froze to death at night.

The British had some knowledge of the local geography because they had found one of Latour's maps in Pensacola. On December 18 two British officers left on a scouting mission to learn more. Hiring several Spanish and Portuguese fishermen as guides, they were led across Lake Borgne to Bayou Bienvenu and then Bayou Mazant. From here they followed a canal, which took them to Jacques Villeré's plantation, located on the east bank of the Mississippi River just eight miles below New Orleans.

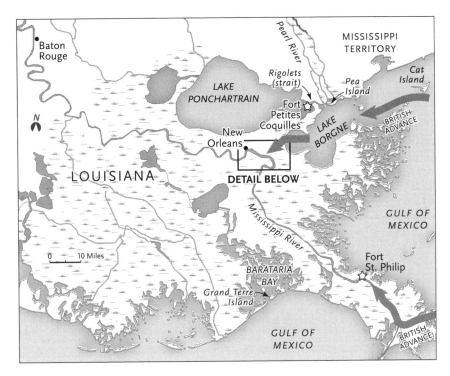

The Louisiana Theater

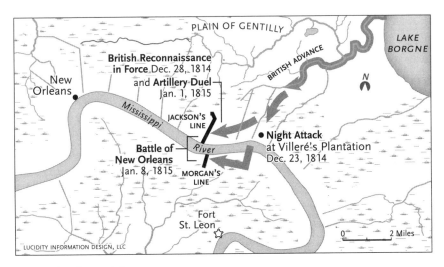

The Battle of New Orleans

The British officers conducted a thorough reconnaissance of the region without being spotted. They reported back to their superiors that this line of approach was unobstructed, and, no less important, it appeared to be completely unguarded. How this approach had escaped Jackson's order to block all approaches is unclear, although it was probably because the Villerés did not want to lose a transportation route that they often used and that they assumed the British would never discover. A militia guard of nine men was sent to a fishing village to guard the route, but these men arrived only after the British had completed their reconnaissance.

With knowledge of the route in hand, a British advance party—1,600 men commanded by Colonel William Thornton (who had spearheaded the attack at Bladensburg outside of Washington the previous summer)—headed for the Villeré plantation, using the limited number of small boats available. They reached their destination at noon on December 23. En route they captured the militia party in the fishing village. They also captured some 30 militiamen who were at the plantation. The only man to escape was Villeré's son, Gabriel, who fled out a back window and raced to New Orleans to alert Jackson. Young Villeré confirmed other reports that Jackson had received that the British had arrived in force just south of the Crescent City.

The British used Villeré's plantation home as their headquarters for the rest of the campaign. Major General John Keane soon arrived to take command. He was far less experienced than the other British generals en route—Pakenham, Samuel Gibbs, and John Lambert—and when he heard reports that inflated Jackson's strength, he chose to wait for reinforcements. Some students of the campaign have argued that by not attacking New Orleans immediately he missed the best British opportunity for victory. Although an attack would have caught Jackson by surprise, Old Hickory had his best troops in the city, and given his coolness in all the crises he had faced to date—most notably when his rear collapsed against the Red Sticks in the Battle of Enotachopco Creek—it is hard to believe that he would not have risen to the occasion if Keane had attacked now.

Jackson was surprised to learn that the British were just a few miles south of the city. Even though he suspected that this was a diversion in favor of a major British attack farther north, he always preferred action to delay and thus decided to strike the British force anyway. He quickly assembled 1,800 men and that night marched them to within a mile of Villeré's plantation. Jackson was supported by the *Carolina*, which had quietly sailed downriver until the British camp was within range of its guns. Although there had been some light skirmishing between American scouts and British pickets earlier in the day, the British were convinced that no force of "Dirty Shirts" would dare attack.

At 7:30 p.m. the *Carolina* opened fire, catching the British by surprise. George R. Gleig, a Scottish junior officer who later became the chaplain-general of the British army, described the scene: "Flash, flash, flash, came from the river; the roar of cannon followed, and the light of her own broadside displayed to us an enemy's vessel at anchor near the opposite bank, and pouring a perfect shower of grape and round shot into the camp."[4] Later the *Carolina* was joined by the *Louisiana*, which kept up a steady stream of artillery fire from farther upriver.

About ten minutes after the *Carolina* opened fire, Jackson attacked from the east along the river. The British were unaware of his presence; for a second time that night they were caught by surprise. The fighting that followed was confusing. The lines were not clearly drawn, and darkness, fog, and smoke made it difficult to distinguish friend from foe. There were some casualties from friendly fire on both sides, and the combat was at such close quarters that there were many bayonet wounds.

Jackson had brought two fieldpieces, which inflicted considerable damage on the British. Although the British nearly captured them, Jackson, who was in the thick of things, inspired his men, and the guns remained in American hands. After the battle was under way, General Coffee attacked with Tennessee riflemen, who inflicted a murderous fire on the British right. But with ever more British reinforcements pouring into the area from Pea Island, Coffee withdrew, and at about 9:00 p.m. Jackson broke off the engagement.

Because Jackson had withdrawn and the British held on to the ground, General Keane claimed victory in the Night Attack, which is also known as the Battle of Villeré's Plantation. But Jackson had the better claim. The British had sustained heavier losses—275 to 215—and they now knew they were facing troops who were willing to fight led by a skillful and aggressive commander. For those British who assumed that they could sweep any resistance aside (as they had at Bladensburg), the entire battle must have been a sobering experience. Ironically, among the prisoners that Jackson took was Major Samuel Mitchell of the 95th Regiment, who had taken part in the campaign against Washington the previous August.

The British Reconnaissance in Force (December 28, 1814)

Jackson had planned to renew the attack the next day (Christmas Eve), but so many British troops were arriving that he decided it would be ill-advised. Instead, with his army now behind Rodriguez Canal, a 4 foot deep and 10 foot wide ditch that had once powered a mill, Jackson ordered Latour to develop an earthen defensive line that would extend from the river in the west to a cypress swamp in the east. Jackson's local white troops considered this kind of manual labor beneath them, but the work went on, and slaves were conscripted to help.

Jackson also ordered that the river levee be cut south of the British position. When the river was high, as it sometimes was in winter and always in the spring, this would flood the entire plain that the British occupied. The water was indeed high, and it ran into the plain but did not remain there for very long. The level of the Mississippi dropped, and the water drained back into the river. So even though the flood annoyed the British, it did not last.

Throughout this period of intense activity, Jackson rarely slept and never took a regular meal. On one occasion, he reportedly went three or four days without much sleep, no doubt relying instead on an occasional catnap. He also ate sparingly, sometimes while on his horse and always as he continued to conduct whatever business was at hand. And if Jackson did not sleep, he tried to keep the enemy from sleeping, too. The two American ships in the river harassed the British with long-range fire, and Tennessee sharpshooters and Choctaw Indians picked off British pickets—a form of partisan warfare that the British considered little better than assassination.

On Christmas day, two days after the Night Attack, Major General Edward Pakenham arrived to take command. He was accompanied by Major General Samuel Gibbs and several staff officers as well as 3,000 men. To deal with the two U.S. warships, Keane had already ordered the construction on the shoreline of a battery of guns that ultimately included two 5.5-inch howitzers and a 5.5-inch mortar together with a furnace to heat shot.

On December 27, the British opened fire with hot shot that soon set the *Carolina* on fire in many places. With fire near the powder magazine, the ship had to be abandoned, and shortly thereafter she blew up, shaking the ground for miles around. British morale was given a momentary boost, while American morale plummeted. Although the navy had lost a valuable asset, most of the crew had escaped, and they managed to get two of the guns off the ship before it sank. Jackson put these guns and gunners to good use in the line he was constructing. The British also fired on the *Louisiana*, which was farther upstream, but she escaped any significant damage when her boats were used to pull her upriver and out of range.

On December 28, Pakenham decided to test Jackson's line, which was protected by 3,300 men, by advancing with a force of around 4,000 men. Proceeding at dawn in two columns, the British met with heavy fire, partly from the five artillery pieces in Jackson's line but mainly from the *Louisiana*, which unleashed 800 rounds. The British deployed their own fieldpieces, but they were soon neutralized by fire from the U.S. warship. The British also employed Congreve rockets, hoping that this new weapons system would panic the inexperienced American troops, but the rockets failed to have that effect.

A British unit on the right led by Lieutenant Colonel Robert Rennie, one of the rising stars in British service, inflicted casualties on a U.S. unit there, leaving that end of the American line near the swamp exposed. But, rather than risk an infantry assault unsupported by artillery, Pakenham ordered a general withdrawal. In an engagement known as the British Reconnaissance in Force, the overall losses on both sides were light, perhaps 35 for the United States and 55 for the British.

In the midst of the battle, Jackson clashed with the legislature. Many of the older Creoles in that body openly voiced their reservations about putting the fate of the city in the hands of a general whose only claim to fame was that he was a successful Indian fighter. As a result, there was renewed talk about surrendering the city to save it from destruction. When an aide informed Jackson of the talk, he was skeptical but told Claiborne to investigate, and if the report proved true, "to blow them up."[5]

Instead, Claiborne shut down the legislative meeting hall and put a guard there to ensure that it remained closed, at least for the time being. Members of the legislature were furious, but there was nothing they could do about it until Claiborne lifted the guard several days later, when the legislature resumed its sessions. The episode further poisoned Claiborne's relationship with the legislature, and now Jackson was embroiled. Jackson's relationship with the legislative body only got worse.

The Artillery Duel (January 1, 1815)

The British Reconnaissance in Force had convinced Jackson that he needed to strengthen his line. A week earlier Jean Lafitte had suggested that the eastern end of the line was vulnerable because it did not extend deep enough into the swamp, and Rennie's attack seemed to confirm this. Accordingly, Jackson ordered the city searched for entrenching tools and drafted slaves to work on the line so that it now extended deep into the swamp and angled back toward the city. To get around the U.S. line via the cypress swamp was now nearly impossible. Rennie, who saw the swamp, described it as "being very boggy, deep, thick, and difficult to penetrate through."[6] Jackson also strengthened the rest of his line and, as a hedge against disaster, ordered two additional lines established closer to the city so that his men could fall back to new positions if necessary.

The recent engagements had convinced Patterson that his naval artillery was too vulnerable in the *Louisiana* because the powerful pull of the current made it difficult to control the ship. So he moved some of his guns to the western shore (where they could be protected by earthworks) and gave the rest to Jackson. The *Louisiana* was then moved farther upriver and out of harm's way. Jackson put the naval guns to good use in his line. On the west bank, Jackson sought to protect Patterson's new battery by ordering earthworks to be erected and assigning troops to defend them.

After the Reconnaissance in Force, Pakenham's troops had withdrawn two miles south of the American line, but they continued to suffer sniper fire from American and Indian sharpshooters. Given the stout resistance that the British had encountered in the Reconnaissance in Force, Pakenham concluded that his best bet was to use heavy guns to create a breach in Jackson's line. His top two staff officers, Lieutenant Colonel Alexander Dickson and Lieutenant Colonel John Fox Burgoyne, concurred. Hence, Pakenham turned to Cochrane for some big naval guns, 18- and 24-pounders, together with their ammunition.

Under the best of circumstances, moving this heavy ordnance was no easy task, but in this case the lack of the right equipment made it much harder. The British had no lifting gear except on their ships and few draft animals, and they lacked the right kind of stout, shallow-draft boats they needed to move the heavy ordnance through the swamps and bayous. It took a great deal of time and muscle to get the big guns first into rowboats and then later into canoes, which were dragged through the muddy swamp to a place where they could be carted in wagons to the British camp. Once the heavy guns had arrived in the camp, they still needed to be hauled into place and mounted on carriages.

Even with this heroic effort, Pakenham did not have everything he needed for the operation. The cartridge cases from the fleet were defective, and the British had to commandeer sheets and curtains from nearby houses for cloth that could serve the purpose. The amount of ammunition brought up fell far short of what was needed for a major artillery campaign, and there was no good way to protect the batteries from U.S. counter-battery fire. Because the water table was just below the surface of the ground, the British could not dig conventional earthworks. Instead, they filled sugar casks with the available earth, but these were neither strong enough nor tall enough to offer much protection.

Under Dickson's supervision, the British were able to set up five artillery and two rocket batteries plus a furnace to heat shot. The artillery batteries consisted of 24 guns: four 24-pound carronades (which fired slow-moving round shot with great force), ten 18-pound cannon, three 5.5-inch mortars (which fired explosive shells, often filled with muskets balls as well as powder), and seven smaller fieldpieces. Most of the firepower was in the main battery, which was located on the British right about 800 yards from the American line. The British had enough artillery but not enough ammunition for the sort of sustained bombardment of Jackson's line that they needed to make.

Jackson now had eight batteries in his line. The batteries, manned mostly by U.S. Army and Navy personnel with an assist from the Baratarians and Louisiana militia, consisted of 14 guns: one 32-pounder, three 24-pounders, two 18-pounders, three 12-pounders, and five smaller fieldpieces. Jackson could also count on three guns on the west bank: one 24-pounder and two 12-pounders. The river was only a half-mile wide here, so these guns could reach the east bank. The British had a distinct edge in firepower, but the Americans had a far greater advantage in their stockpile of ammunition, and this would prove decisive in the artillery duel that followed.

Early on January 1, 1815, under the cover of darkness, British troops moved to within 500 yards of the American line to prepare for an assault. Fog delayed the British artillery barrage until 10:00 a.m. The first target was Jackson's headquarters in the McCarty plantation house. Although the house was hit by scores of balls, shells, and rockets within ten minutes, miraculously neither Jackson (who was inside) nor anyone else was injured. The British next took aim at the American batteries and did some damage to them, but most of their rounds either overshot their mark or landed harmlessly in the American earthworks.

Although caught unprepared, the Americans recovered quickly, and their counter-battery fire soon told. The sugar casks provided little protection to the British guns or their crews, and one battery was knocked completely out of action. More importantly, the British eventually ran out of ammunition. By noon their fire had lessened, and it ended altogether at 3:00 p.m. "Our fire slackened every moment," recalled a British officer, "that of the Americans became every moment more terrible, till at length, after not more than two hours and a half of firing, our batteries were all silenced."[7]

The British assumed that the American left was still vulnerable. This was the only part of Jackson's line that British infantry attacked during the artillery duel. However, the line had been extended and strengthened, and the British were easily repulsed. When the British pulled back, they left their artillery in place, but since the Americans made no attempt to seize it, they were able to return during the ensuing night and either disable or retrieve it. The plain was so steeped in mud that Pakenham had to call upon his entire army working in 100-man shifts to haul off the big guns. Dragging the guns through the mud, recalled one British naval officer, "was the dirtiest and the most fatiguing job I ever was engaged in."[8] The United States had clearly prevailed in the Artillery Duel (also known as the Battle of Rodriguez Canal), but casualties were light. The British lost 75 men, the Americans about 35.

With the conclusion of the Artillery Duel, the opposing armies had engaged in three battles in ten days, and Jackson had won each time. General Pakenham's options for what to do next were limited. He could withdraw to find a better place to attack, but this would be an admission of defeat and no doubt would undermine the morale of his army. Hemmed in by the river and swamp, his only alternative was a frontal assault against Jackson's line. This was risky, but it was the only course of action that the British general considered feasible.

Some British officers were skeptical of their chances. One junior officer later said: "I do not remember ever looking for the first signs of daybreak with more intense anxiety than on this eventful morning."[9] Others, however, welcomed an opportunity to bring the campaign to a successful conclusion and show the "Dirty Shirts" just how well a veteran British army, fresh from the battlefields of Europe, could perform against a bunch of amateurs. Surely an army that had defeated Napoleon's finest could route a backwoods force with so little training and experience.

More American Preparations

In the wake of the artillery duel, Jackson continued to work on his main line as well as his two lines to the rear. To make it more difficult for the enemy to get to his line, Jackson deepened the Rodriguez Canal and then flooded it with 30 thirty inches of water by cutting through the river levee. Slaves not only did much of this work but also brought in earth from elsewhere to strengthen the line. Everyone working on the line had to endure the cold and wet weather.

When completed, Jackson's line resembled the giant levee that had been built parallel to the Mississippi River to prevent flooding, but this line was perpendicular to the river and varied in height and depth. In some places, the line was as much as 20 feet thick, although far to the east, in the swamp, it was only 4 feet thick. The height of the line also varied, ranging from 4 to 8 feet. Where it was high, a fire step enabled the men to shoot over the top. Since the canal was 4 feet deep, anyone standing in it was well below the top of the line. Both sides of the wall were lined with fencing taken from miles around to keep the earth in place. Next to the river in front of the line, Jackson ordered the construction of a small redoubt so that field artillery could fire parallel to the line on any enemy troops who came near. This defensive work was never completed.

On January 4 some 2,400 volunteer militia under the command of Major General John Thomas arrived from Kentucky, bringing Jackson's total strength to over 10,000 men. Less than a third of the Kentuckians brought weapons, and some of the ones they had did not work. Rifles that Jackson had ordered the previous August had left Pittsburgh on a flatboat in November, but except for a portion commandeered by some Tennessee troops on their way to New Orleans, the weapons did not arrive until a week after the coming battle was over. As a result, Jackson did not have enough shoulder weapons to arm all of his men.

The Kentucky soldiers also arrived without proper clothing or blankets. The legislature appropriated $6,000 and the public donated another $16,000 so that blankets and woolen cloth could be purchased. The women of New Orleans then turned the material into wearing apparel. The mayor also quietly donated a cache of 500 small arms kept in reserve in case of a slave revolt. The best of the Kentucky troops were put on the left side of the American line under Brigadier General John Adair, where the main British assault was expected.

Lieutenant Colonel John Davis led some of the Kentuckians to the west bank, where they joined other militia from Kentucky and Louisiana under Brigadier General David B. Morgan, an inexperienced officer in the Louisiana militia. Morgan's total strength on the west bank was about 800 men, but most were poorly armed and trained and had little confidence in Morgan's leadership. Moreover, when Patterson established additional batteries on the west bank to harass the British, Morgan abandoned a short line designed by Jackson's engineers for a much longer one downriver so that he could protect Patterson's batteries. The new line, however, was completely exposed at the west end, so that it was vulnerable to either being rolled up by an advancing enemy or bypassed altogether. Morgan asked Jackson for more men to properly cover his right flank, but Jackson, who correctly anticipated that the main British attack would come on the east bank, was unwilling to weaken his line to accommodate Morgan's needs. Jackson simply ordered Morgan "to maintain his position at all hazards."[10]

More British Preparations

Jackson's snipers continued to harass the British by day and night. Patterson's artillery on the west bank periodically took aim at targets of opportunity in or near the British camp, including a number of houses that the British army was using. The harassing fire meant that despite the weather the British could not take comfort in fires at night. Nor did they enjoy decent meals. With the food in the area now exhausted, they were reduced to eating provisions from the fleet, horse meat, and the abundant sugar. Disease, always the biggest enemy of armies in the field, also stalked the British troops, especially those from the West Indies.

With the lack of success on the battlefield and the lack of comforts in the camp, British morale began to sink, and the desertion rate rose. Pakenham doubted he could attack again until 2,100 men under Major General John Lambert arrived. The last of these reinforcements, which included two crack regiments from the Peninsular War, reached the British camp on January 6. Each soldier brought a cannon ball in his knapsack to replenish the supply on the front lines. When a boatload of these troops overturned on Lake Borgne, the extra weight carried 17 men to the bottom. A midshipman and four seamen also drowned in this incident. Those troops who made it safely to Pakenham's camp raised his total strength to over 10,000 men.

To prepare for the final assault, the British built scaling ladders from green wood taken from the cypress swamp and fascines (bundles of sticks that would provide secure footing across damp ground) from sugar cane. The artillery was repaired, and the artillery ammunition brought up by the recent troops was distributed. At last there was enough of this ammunition to serve the needs of the operation.

In the meantime, Admiral Cochrane suggested that the British deepen, widen, and extend Villeré's Canal so that they could move watercraft to the river. This would allow them to transport a force across the river that might be able to seize control of the west bank and fire on Jackson's line from that direction. The work on the canal was extraordinarily demanding and tedious. When the project was done, it was not clear that a dam built across the canal would hold when the levee along the river was breached to allow the canal to fill with water. Nor was it possible to bring up enough boats to move the large force that would be assigned to the mission on the west bank of the river.

The Battle of New Orleans (January 8, 1815)

By January 7 the British were ready for their main attack. No one on either side doubted the importance of the coming battle. Just about everyone assumed it would be the decisive engagement of the campaign. Though each side had over 10,000 men in service somewhere in the Louisiana theater, less than half this number took part in the main battle on the east bank. The rest were on the west bank, were being held in reserve, or were deployed to other sites in the theater.

Pakenham planned to attack on the east bank with about 5,300 men supported by four 24-pounders and four 18-pounders. Jackson had around 4,700 men in his line supported by eight batteries that included one 32-pounder, three 24-pounders, and two 18-pounders. He could also count on some support from Patterson's three batteries on the east bank, which now included three 24-pounders and six 12-pounders. Jackson had a big advantage in the firepower of his artillery and an even bigger advantage in the strength of his defensive works. This double advantage would prove decisive in the battle that ensued.

The British plan of attack was simple. One force would cross to the west bank, march north along the river, storm the U.S. position, and then turn the naval guns there against Jackson's main line across the river. At the same time, the British on the east bank would launch the principal attack. A detachment was expected to seize the incomplete U.S. redoubt near the river in front of Rodriguez Canal. This was to serve as a diversion and also prevent U.S. artillery in the redoubt from firing on the main British force, which was to focus on Jackson's left (near the cypress swamp), where his line was considered weakest. The British artillery batteries were to take aim at the batteries in Jackson's line only after the British infantry got close enough to use their muskets, at about 150 yards.

The British plan was not unreasonable, especially given the quality of the British troops, but there were too many variables. The result was an unmitigated disaster. The British could not overcome the many obstacles they faced: a lack of boats, an unruly river, uncooperative weather, and, most of all, Jackson's stout defenses and firepower, especially from his artillery.

Bloodbath on the East Bank

On the night of January 7–8, British work parties advanced toward Jackson's line to prepare earthworks for artillery, and before dawn the eight big guns were moved into place. None of this work was easy, the incessant rains having turned the ground into a sea of mud. Around 4:00 a.m. some 5,300 British troops trudged through the muck to their assigned places near the artillery, perhaps 500 yards from Jackson's line. Before them lay more mud and then the flooded Rodriguez Canal.

None of the British preparations came as a surprise to anyone on the American side of the line. Jackson learned from British deserters and other sources that the attack was planned for Sunday, January 8. Old Hickory had risen from bed at 1:00 a.m. that morning and headed for the front line, where he checked to make sure that all was in order. By the time he got there, the British preparations could be distinctly heard by those behind the American line. In the ensuing battle, Jackson initially moved up and down the line (on horseback and in full uniform), encouraging his men, who occasionally

Benson J. Lossing, a New York artist and amateur historian who spent the 1850s visiting War of 1812 sites, prepared this sketch of the Battle of New Orleans based on a view that Jackson's principal engineer, Arsène Latour, had produced shortly after the battle. The sketch captured the smoke and the extent of action on Jackson's right but not the intense fighting at the other end of the line, where the British sustained their heaviest casualties. The sketch also understated the height and depth of Jackson's line. (Benson J. Lossing, *Pictorial Field-Book of the War of 1812* [New York, 1868])

responded with cheers. Then he took a position in the center of the line that was slightly elevated so that he could take in (smoke and daylight permitting) the entire field. To keep up American morale, he ordered a band behind the center of the line to play music continuously until the battle was over.

Thornton was supposed to cross the river the previous day after dark, but the dam the British had built across Villeré's Canal had collapsed when the levee was breached to fill it with river water. This meant the British had no easy way to move the boats to Thornton at the river's edge. A few were dragged overland, but this put Thornton far behind schedule and with only a fraction of the boats he needed. He did not leave the east bank until the morning of January 8, and he got only about half of his 1,200-man force across the river. As it happened, he had enough troops to do the job, but he had fallen so far behind schedule that he could not offer any support to the main British attack on the other side.

The lack of support from the west bank was not the only problem the British faced. Because of a breakdown in communications, the fascines and ladders did not reach the front in a timely fashion, although it probably did not matter because in all likelihood heavy U.S. small arms would have cut down anyone who got atop Jackson's earthworks. Pakenham was unaware of this problem, but he knew that he was unlikely to get any help from the west bank. Nevertheless, he decided to go ahead with the assault anyway, confident (or at least hopeful) that his men could still do the job. He did not want to delay the start of the attack beyond dawn because the men in forward positions were now exposed to fire from Jackson's batteries, and daylight would also expose them to fire from the American naval guns on the west bank. Hence, he stayed on schedule, ordering a Congreve rocket fired into the air at 6:00 a.m. as a signal for the attack to begin.

The British force by the river, just three light companies accompanied by 100 West India troops and some detached artillery soldiers, led by Lieutenant Colonel Robert Rennie, had to contend with artillery fire from Patterson's guns on the west bank. Although firing blindly because fog initially covered the battlefield, these guns took a toll on the British. Rennie's men nonetheless succeeded in overrunning the U.S. redoubt. Rennie then mounted the U.S. wall just beyond the redoubt and called for his men to follow, but he was cut down by small arms fire. Without reinforcements, the remaining troops had to withdraw after taking heavy casualties. A few other British soldiers who made it to the top of the wall were killed or wounded, and one officer who made it over the wall was quickly surrounded and captured.

The artillery crews in Jackson's line also had to contend with fog, although they could see well enough to open fire on the British when they began their advance some 500 yards out. Fire from these batteries became increasingly effective as the British got nearer to the American line and the fog began to dissipate. Alexander Dickson, head of the British artillery, expressed regret that the attack had not begun earlier when it was still dark "as the Enemy would not have directed their fire with such certainty."[11] As it was, the effect of this fire was devastating. A single round of canister (a large can of musket balls) from the big 32-pounder in one of Jackson's batteries swept away the entire center of the attacking force, reportedly causing some 200 casualties.

When the British got within 300 yards of Jackson's line, the Kentucky and Tennessee riflemen opened fire. British troops who got within 150 yards were also fired on by muskets, which were more numerous in Jackson's line than rifles. Most of the muskets were loaded with "buck and ball" (a musket ball and two or three buckshot), which made them more likely to hit something but less lethal. The combined effect of the big guns and small arms from Jackson's line was astonishing. According to a British veteran of the Napoleonic Wars, it was "the most murderous [fire] I ever beheld before or since."[12]

Most of Jackson's men with rifles or muskets were organized into ranks, ranging from two to four. After one rank fired, it was supposed to withdraw to reload while another rank stepped forward to fire. In fact, this scheme broke down almost immediately, and every man fired at his own pace. But the effect was the same: heavy and sustained small arms fire. And because Americans all along the line were protected by their earthworks, the British did not have much of a target to respond to.

In those parts of the line that were more than 5 feet high, many men simply remained under cover, raised their weapons above their heads, and fired blindly without looking. Even when the fog lifted, it was still not very light out, and the smoke from the black powder used covered much of the battlefield so that even those Americans looking over the line were often firing blindly. As a Kentucky soldier remembered it, "It was so dark that little could be seen until just about the time the battle ceased. The morning had dawned to be sure, but the smoke was so thick that everything seemed to be covered up in it."[13] A good breeze might have cleared the smoke, but that does not appear to have happened on this day.

Major General Samuel Gibbs was mortally wounded trying to rally his men. In much agony, he died the next day. Shortly after Gibbs was hit, Pakenham rode up. He was shot in the knee, and after one horse was shot out from under him, he commandeered another and was reportedly "cut asunder by a cannon ball."[14] General Keane was also seriously wounded, although he survived. The units on the British right, particularly Gibbs's brigade and the 93rd Scottish Regiment, took particularly heavy casualties. After less than half an hour, the carnage was so great that the British withdrew. The rifles and muskets in Jackson's line continued to fire for another hour and a half until Jackson ordered a cease fire at 8:00 a.m.

Rout on the West Bank

On the west bank, things went much better for the British although what happened there had no impact on the main battle. Thornton was eight hours behind schedule, and he lost still more time when the current carried his boats farther downriver than he anticipated. He had just got his men across the river when he saw the flashes of cannon fire on the other side, indicating

Major General Edward Pakenham in full regalia. This portrait captures the supreme confidence of the officer who commanded British soldiers in the campaign to seize New Orleans. As a boy Jackson had refused to clean a British officer's boots, for which he received a sabre slash that left him scarred for life. Pakenham was killed in battle. (Painting by T. Heaphy. Alcée Fortier, *History of Louisiana* [New York, 1904])

that the battle there was under way. With some 600 men he raced north dragging three barges that carried fieldpieces and Congreve rockets. A half hour later he reached an American advance party of less than 400 poorly armed and trained Louisiana and Kentucky militia.

The Kentucky militia delivered several volleys before one of their officers arrived on the scene and ordered them to pull back to the main line. This was evidently passed on to the French-speaking Louisiana militia as "*Sauve qui peut*," which translated freely means, "Every man for himself." The Louisiana militia quickly fled, and these men were never thereafter a factor. The Kentuckians fell back in some disorder to Morgan's main line. Although the newcomers deployed on Morgan's right, away from the river, that end of the line was only waist high and remained exposed because it did not extend far enough inland.

Thornton momentarily halted his advance and used a handheld telescope to assess Morgan's line. Since it was weakest in the west, he concentrated his attack at that end of the line. Morgan ordered several small fieldpieces fired at the advancing British who, relying on bayonets and cutlasses, stormed his position, overrunning the poorly defended right side of his line. During the attack, Thornton's men fired several Congreve rockets. They did little harm but probably contributed to the growing sense of panic that gripped the Kentucky defenders.

With the British upon them, the Kentuckians in the west broke and ran, and they were soon followed by the others in Morgan's line. About a half mile to the rear, Patterson's batteries were now exposed. The naval commander considered firing on the retreating Kentuckians who were racing toward him but instead ordered a withdrawal. He left his naval guns, not all of which had been spiked.

The British pursued Morgan's retreating troops for two miles and then returned to take control of the ground the Americans had occupied. A howitzer the British captured carried the inscription "Taken at the surrender of Yorktown, 1781." Jackson sent several officers across to assume command and retake the ground, but they found the militia spooked and uncooperative. Fortunately for the United States, Thornton's success came too late to help Pakenham. In the wake of the British disaster on the east bank, Thornton was ordered to withdraw.

Cease-fire

With Pakenham and Gibbs dead and Keane wounded, General Lambert assumed command. He summoned a council of war, and most of the officers present expressed opposition to renewing the attack. Lambert agreed. He sent a flag of truce to Jackson, asking for a temporary suspension of hostilities to tend to the wounded and bury the dead. Jackson consented but with stipulations. To prevent the British from gaining an advantage on the west bank, Jackson insisted that neither side reinforce it; and to prevent the British from learning more about his defenses, he insisted that Americans take charge of the dead and wounded within 300 yards of his line. Lambert agreed to these conditions.

The cease-fire began the next day at 10:00 a.m. and ran until 2:00 p.m. By the time the armistice went into effect, many of the British wounded had made it back to their camp or had been carried across the American line. Americans had also begun to scour the battlefield for souvenirs and valuables, picking up small arms, swords, scabbards, personal possessions, and clothing, especially boots (always a coveted prize). This kind of looting was common at the time and was often initiated by eager soldiers even before a battle was over.

The engagement on January 8, 1815—which was *the* Battle of New Orleans—was the biggest and bloodiest single engagement of the War of 1812. Most of the damage had been done at the ends of Jackson's lines. The artillery batteries had been especially lethal, but small arms also took a toll. One American observer said the battlefield was a terrible sight to behold, "with dead and wounded all laying in heaps," and all in scarlet British uniforms.[15] Another said the British were in every possible position. "Some had their heads shot off, some their legs, some their arms. Some were laughing, some crying, some groaning, and some screaming."[16] A British officer who toured the battlefield was stunned by what he saw. "Of all the sights I ever witnessed," he ruefully noted, "that which met me there was beyond comparison the most shocking and the most humiliating. Within the narrow compass of a few hundred yards were gathered together nearly a thousand bodies, all of them arrayed in British uniforms."[17]

Just about everyone was stunned by the disparity in casualties. The British lost over 2,000 men, including at least 850 who were killed or mortally wounded and another 500 who were captured. Among the dead and wounded were 90 officers, including three generals and seven colonels. Many of those captured had taken refuge under the American wall or hit the ground to escape the murderous American fire. Most had then surrendered, one claiming that he did not try to escape because *"these d—d Yankee riflemen can pick a squirrel's eye out as far as they can see it."*[18]

The Americans carried the British dead near their line to the armistice line 300 yards out, and the British began the laborious task of burying the dead. Although normally the dead were interred in long trenches, in this case some 200 bodies were tossed into a huge hole. "The bodies [were] hurled in as fast as we could bring them," recalled a British officer.[19] Rain later washed away what little soil covered the bodies. The rank of several senior officers, including Pakenham, Gibbs, and Rennie, entitled them to be buried on British soil. Hence, their remains were shipped home in barrels of spirits.

Jackson's losses by contrast, were modest: only 71 killed and wounded, and only 13 in the main engagement on the east side of the river. "The vast disparity of loss," said a Washington newspaper, "would stagger credulity itself, were it not confirmed by a whole army of witnesses."[20] In the four battles of the campaign, the British had sustained 2,450 killed, wounded, captured, or missing, while Jackson's losses were only about 350.

The Aftermath of Victory

Jackson naturally received the lion's share of praise for the outcome of the Battle of New Orleans, and it was fully deserved, as his leadership, determination, and vision produced the victory. On the British side, Thornton, who was wounded again (as he had been at Bladensburg) came out of the battle with the most credit for his success on the east bank.

Both sides looked for someone to blame for their failures. The British blamed the disaster on the east bank on Lieutenant Colonel Thomas Mullins, a brave but unpopular officer who was charged with getting the fascines and ladders to the front lines before the attack. The battle began before the equipment had arrived; although it was eventually brought forward, it was too late. It is doubtful whether the equipment would have made any difference, but Mullins was nonetheless court-martialed. Although charged with cowardice, he had shown such exceptional bravery during the battle, moving ahead to Jackson's line even though wounded, that this charge did not stick. He was ultimately convicted of "neglect of duty" and cashiered from the British army.

Jackson and Patterson blamed the failure on the west bank on Lieutenant Colonel John Davis and the Kentucky militia even though the Louisiana militiamen were probably as culpable. A court of inquiry seemed to absolve just about everyone. The only exception was Major Paul Arnaud, who became the scapegoat for General Morgan's shortcomings. The court attributed the retreat to "the shameful flight of the command of major Arnaud."[21] Jackson, however, never changed his view that the Kentuckians were at fault. The Kentuckians never forgave Jackson and, in turn, blamed the Louisianans. This led to a three-way feud that persisted for years. John Adair, who actually served with distinction in Jackson's main line, became the leading defender of the Kentucky troops on the west bank. In 1818 the public debate became so heated that he and Jackson very nearly dueled.

The Battle of New Orleans was the last major battle of the War of 1812, but by no means the last battle. The British remained in place for another ten days while they worked on a makeshift road to get back to Lake Borgne, where boats could ferry them to the fleet. During the lull the British camp and pickets continued to be harassed with artillery and sniper fire. Even after they had departed, U.S. raiding parties were sent to annoy them while they waited at Lake Borgne to return to the fleet. There was also an exchange of prisoners.

Jackson wisely made no attempt to do more than harass the British during this period. He had won the battle and the campaign, and New Orleans was saved. There was no point in risking defeat by attacking what was still a fine British army that was receiving reinforcements from Great Britain and Canada. When the British departed, they left 80 of their most seriously wounded behind. Americans gave them the same care they gave their own wounded. Another exchange of prisoners followed in early February. Jackson insisted on returning some prisoners who had been persuaded to desert, believing that it was improper to recruit those in American hands and expressing hope to the British that they would not be punished.

Jackson sought the return of some runaway slaves who left with the British, but as long as the war continued he would not permit locals to send a special delegation to seek their return. Such a mission, he told Governor Claiborne, would be "a degradation of that national character of which we boast."[22] On the other hand, Jackson was happy to comply with General Keane's request to return a sword that he lost on the battlefield. "*I have sent it to him,*" he said, "although a trophy of war [it is] still . . . greater to be able to yield it to him!" "British pride," he added, is "much humbled."[23]

The day after the British left Louisiana, Jackson asked the local Catholic prelate, Abbé Guillaume Dubourg, to conduct a public service of thanksgiving. Jackson marched the bulk of his army back into New Orleans, where a triumphal arch had been erected in the main square. After Dubourg delivered a speech thanking Jackson and the Almighty for preserving New Orleans, he presented the commanding general with a laurel wreath. The party then entered the cathedral for the service, after which, in a city that was now brilliantly illuminated, a festival of eating and drinking took place that lasted all night.

Fort St. Philip and Fort Bowyer

Admiral Cochrane was as yet unwilling to give up on the campaign. He decided after the Battle of New Orleans to try to force Fort St. Philip to submit by sending a squadron upriver to bombard the post. Because it was surrounded by swamps, the fort could not be assaulted by land. Hence, the British had to rely on naval artillery. The squadron included two bomb ships carrying 13-inch mortars that fired huge explosive shells. The fort, which was under the command of Major Walter H. Overton, had been strengthened in the fall, and much more work had been done after Jackson's arrival. The post had thus become a formidable target.

In a ten-day bombardment that lasted from January 9 to January 18, the British expended 10 tons of powder firing 70 tons of ammunition. Most of the fire came from 5-ton 13-inch mortars that were nearly 4,000 yards away and fired huge explosive shells that weighed nearly 200 pounds. The fort did not have fuses for its own 13-inch mortar shells until near the end of the engagement, when it finally responded with counter-battery fire. By then the British had concluded that Fort St. Philip (like Fort McHenry) was too well built to be reduced. They gave up their attack and withdrew down the river. The ten-day bombardment had produced only nine U.S. casualties.

Next the British launched an amphibious attack on Fort Bowyer in Mobile Bay. This time, unlike the previous September, the British devoted enough resources to succeed. On February 11, 1815, the fort was surrounded on three sides by the Royal Navy, and some 5,000 men under General Lambert were landed on shore. Lambert got his field artillery within 100 yards of the fort and opened fire. Since Major William Lawrence had only 375 men to defend the fort, he bowed to the inevitable and surrendered. Jackson took a dim view of Lawrence's surrender, but a military court exonerated him.

The fall of Fort Bowyer left Mobile exposed. It is unclear whether General Winchester, who was charged with protecting the city, would have tried to defend it. He was never put to the test because on February 14 a schooner reached the British at Fort Bowyer with news that their government had signed and ratified the peace treaty. Even Cochrane, who still had visions of retrieving the situation on the Gulf Coast with additional operations, had to concede that the war was now virtually over since it was unlikely that the U.S. government would refuse to ratify the treaty.

Jackson's Iron Grip

Jackson, by contrast, was much slower to acknowledge the growing signs of peace or to loosen his grip on his troops or the city. In September 1814 militia from Tennessee who were garrisoning Fort Jackson were short of food and afflicted with disease. Becoming increasingly unruly, they broke into the commissary for provisions and then left for home. Other men joined them from nearby forts. The men, 200 in all, had gone home because they thought they could not be required to serve for more than three months.

Three months had always been the maximum under the Militia Act of 1795. Congress had authorized six-month tours in 1814, but it remained unclear whether the men had been called out for the longer tour. Jackson had no doubt that the men had been called out for six months and ordered them arrested. By then many had returned voluntarily. "A few being shot," Jackson said prophetically, "will learn the balance that they have a country and they have rights to defend."[24] All were tried by a military court in Mobile in December 1814. Most were convicted of desertion and sentenced to forfeit part of their pay, make up for lost time, and then be drummed out of camp with their heads partly shaved.

Jackson later pardoned these men, but the six ringleaders—a sergeant and five privates—were not so lucky. They were convicted of mutiny (and in some cases also desertion) and were sentenced to be shot. Jackson approved the verdicts on January 22. This was two weeks after the Battle of New Orleans, a battle that Jackson conceded was "fatal to [British] hopes," and four days after the British had departed from Louisiana. The executions were scheduled to take place at Mobile on February 21, 1815.[25] By this time the British had taken Fort Bowyer but, having learned of the peace treaty, had suspended military operations.

General Winchester, who was in command at Mobile, knew nothing of peace and in any case was unlikely to defy Jackson or to delay carrying out his orders—especially with the British on his doorstep. On the appointed date the six men were blindfolded and forced to kneel on their coffins. They were then executed by a firing squad of 36 men. The following day, news of preliminary peace reached Mobile. This grisly and tragic episode attracted little attention at the time because of the excitement generated by the return of peace, but years later it was used by Jackson's enemies to try to block his bid for the presidency.

Jackson also continued to feud with the Creoles in Louisiana. His threat in December to blow up the legislature if there was any further talk of surrendering had not gone down well. In a legislative resolution adopted on February 2 thanking all those who had had a hand in saving the city, Jackson's name was conspicuously absent. Moreover, when the house voted to appropriate $800 for a ceremonial saber for Jackson, the measure went down to defeat in the senate.

Even more galling, Jackson was slow to release militia from service or to lift martial law, which had been in force since December 16, 1814. On January 19, 1815, the day after the British had completed their evacuation and given up their bombardment of Fort St. Philip, Jackson told the secretary of war that "Louisiana is now clear of its enemy" and that he thought it likely that Britain's "last exertions have been made in this quarter, at any rate for the present season."[26] However, Jackson did not share these views with the people of New Orleans. Nor was he willing to lessen his grip when unofficial news of a peace treaty arrived on February 19.

Two days later, when the Louisiana *Gazette* reported that Jackson had received a dispatch from Admiral Cochrane announcing the end of the war and requesting a suspension of hostilities, Jackson publicly denounced the *Gazette* report as inaccurate and made it clear that he would not relax his hold on the city until he received official word that the United States had signed and ratified a peace treaty. This news did not reach New Orleans until nearly mid-March. In the meantime, residents of New Orleans, particularly the French Creoles, were eager to return to private life and found their continued service in militia units both onerous and inexplicable. The outbreak of dysentery and fever in their camps produced considerable suffering, and an order issued by Jackson that prohibited liquor in camp only added to the discontent.

French Creoles started applying to Louis de Tousard, the French consul in New Orleans, for certificates showing that they were French citizens and thus exempt from militia duty. Jackson countersigned a number of these documents, but Tousard (whom Jackson later called "a wicked and dangerous man") was willing to sign applications for just about anyone because he collected a small fee for each one. Soon Jackson was inundated with the documents.[27] In typical Jacksonian style, he responded by ordering all French citizens, including Tousard, to leave New Orleans within three days and to remain at least as far away as Baton Rouge until the war was over or the British had left the area. He also ordered the voting rolls for the most recent election searched on the grounds that anyone who voted was a U.S. citizen and thus obligated to perform militia service.

Jackson's order was the last straw for Louis Louaillier, a prominent and respected member of the legislature, who wrote an angry letter to the Louisiana *Courier* denouncing Jackson. "Are we to restrain our indignation," he asked, "when we remember that these very Frenchmen, who are now exiled, have so powerfully contributed to the preservation of Louisiana?" Even the president, he argued, had no authority to order the citizens of a friendly nation around in this manner. "It is high time," he concluded, that "the laws should resume their empire; that citizens of this State should return to the full enjoyment of their rights."[28]

Louaillier's letter, written in French, was signed "A Citizen of Louisiana of French Origin." Jackson ordered the editor of the paper to disclose the author's identity; he did. Two days later Louaillier was arrested while walking along the levee. When Judge Dominick Hall ordered Louaillier released, Jackson jailed the judge for exciting mutiny in his camp. When John Dick, the U.S. district attorney, sought to secure Hall's release before another judge, Jackson ordered both arrested, although apparently he recalled this order before it was executed. A military court reviewed the charges against Louaillier, which ranged from spying to mutiny, and refused to convict him. Jackson overruled the court and kept the Creole in jail. He released Hall but ordered the judge out of the city until the war was over or the British had left the Gulf Coast.

In the midst of this legal tussle, on March 6, a courier arrived from Washington bearing a packet that was supposed to contain an official letter informing Jackson that a peace treaty had reached the capital. The packet contained no such document. However, the courier did have a letter from the postmaster general ordering all postal officials to facilitate his journey because he bore news of peace. This was not good enough for Jackson to lift martial law, although on the basis of what he had learned he proposed a cease-fire to General Lambert, discharged the Louisiana militia called out in the *levée en masse*, and allowed French citizens (except for Tousard) to return to the city.

The British had been unresponsive to Jackson's appeals for the return of runaway slaves. The commanding general now let a party of Louisiana citizens visit the Royal fleet under a flag of truce to make a personal appeal to the runaways. These appeals fell on deaf ears, and General Lambert refused to compel any slaves to return against their will. The refugees, some 200 in all, preferred freedom and sailed off with the Royal Navy. They were but a small portion of the 4,000 who found freedom by fleeing to British camps or British ships during the War of 1812. Afterwards, they settled as freemen in new homes in Canada, the West Indies, or elsewhere in the British Empire.

A week later, on March 13, official news of peace finally arrived. With this Jackson announced a cessation of hostilities, ended marital law, and pardoned all personnel charged with military offenses. The next day he discharged all militia still in service, sent the volunteers from Kentucky and Tennessee home, and discharged those from Louisiana and the Mississippi Territory. Three days later, on March 17, he relinquished his command to Major General Edmund P. Gaines, who had recently served on the Niagara front.

Jackson Hauled into Court

Louaillier was released, and Hall was now free to return to New Orleans and resume his position on the bench. Several days later the judge charged Jackson with contempt of court for disregarding his writ to release Louaillier and for imprisoning the judge. Jackson sought to defend himself by reading a long paper (prepared by Edward Livingston) that characterized the proceedings against him as both illegal and unconstitutional and that justified the proclamation of martial law. Judge Hall refused to admit the paper as evidence, asserting that the issue was not whether martial law was legal but whether Jackson's treatment of the court was contemptuous. "The only question," asserted Judge Hall, "was whether the Law should bend to the General or the General to the Law."[29]

There were rumors in the city that the Baratarians, who had never liked Judge Hall's interference with their illegal trade, would storm the court and close it down to save Jackson, but this never happened. Rebuffed in his attempt to rest his case on the legality of martial law, Jackson made no further defense. Hall found him guilty and fined him $1,000. Jackson refused to defy the judge and also insisted on paying the fine himself despite offers from supporters. However, in 1844, when the aging and now destitute hero of New Orleans was near death, Congress refunded the fine with interest—$2,733 in all—although only after a bitterly partisan two-year contest.

Jackson's supporters carried him from the court to his carriage. Amid cries of "Vive le General Jackson! Vive le General Jackson!" he rode triumphantly to his quarters. Throngs of people lined the streets to pay tribute along the route, and he periodically stopped to deliver a short address. "Obedience to the laws," he told his admirers, "even when we think them unjustly applied [is] the first duty of a citizen." "[If] my example can teach you this useful lesson I shall not regret the sacrifice it has cost me."[30]

Privately, Jackson simmered over his legal ordeal and refused to allow the matter to drop. He engaged in an unseemly newspaper exchange with Judge Hall and told one correspondent that he had been detained in New Orleans "by a combination of a few Traitors & Tories—with Judge Hall at their head . . . who are much chagrined because the country has been saved from the [British] lion's grasp." Jackson's relationship with Governor Claiborne, never warm, degenerated into open hostility when the governor issued a circular that was critical of Jackson's despotic rule. In his controversy with Judge Hall, Jackson considered the governor "the moving machine behind the curtain." He claimed that Claiborne "will always be filled with faction" and "will abandon principle, and attach himself to Tories & traitors, to raise his popularity regardless of truth or his country's good."[31]

Jackson even went so far as to accuse Claiborne of cowardice, claiming that he was "a perfect old woman . . . hiding himself from the Balls & Rockets of the enemy instead of encouraging the men upon the lines."[32] This charge was unjust. In spite of his lack of military experience, Claiborne insisted on commanding militia called into service, but Jackson was careful to post him to sites where there was no combat. Only belatedly was he ordered to the west bank, but by then the battle was over.

The administration in Washington, which received an earful on Jackson's dictatorial ways from Claiborne, took a dim view of the general's contempt for the law, but it could hardly publicly criticize the now immensely popular hero of New Orleans. Instead, it privately reprimanded Jackson for proclaiming martial law and for using his military authority to block the operation of the courts, suspend freedom of the press, and treat French citizens in such a manner. By the time this reprimand caught up with Jackson, he was back in Tennessee being treated like a conquering hero. He had already moved on to the next phase of his life. A half century later, in *Ex parte Milligan* (1866), the U.S. Supreme Court in another case suggested that, however justified Jackson's proclamation of martial law might have been, it was unconstitutional. "Martial law can never exist," the court said, "where the courts are open, and in the proper and unobstructed exercise of their jurisdiction."[33]

Jackson's Generalship

The Battle of New Orleans was the last battle that Andrew Jackson ever fought. It marked the end of a remarkable run of 14 months in which he never lost a battle. Beginning with his victory at Talladega on November 9, 1813, Jackson won four successive battles over the Red Sticks, culminating in a decisive victory at Horseshoe Bend on March 27–28, 1814. And beginning with the Night Attack on December 23, 1814, Jackson won four successive battles over the British, culminating in his spectacular success in the main battle at New Orleans on January 8, 1815. This run was matched by no one else in the War of 1812, and it was achieved under some of the most challenging conditions that any commander faced.

What accounts for Jackson's success on the battlefield? First, he had a good grasp of strategy and tactics. There is no evidence that he ever read any treatise or manual on war-making. Rather, he relied on intuition and common sense, and this served him well. Whether he was fighting the Creeks or the British, he grasped the big picture and thus knew how best to achieve his campaign objectives. He was also an effective, even master, tactician, deploying his forces on the battlefield in a way that gave him the best chance of victory. Against the Creeks, Jackson knew when to attack (at Talladega and Horseshoe Bend), when to defend (at Emuckfau), when to withdraw and how to do so safely (at Enotachopco Creek). Similarly, against the British he knew when to attack (at night at Villeré's Plantation) and when to defend (in the three ensuing engagements at New Orleans).

Jackson made superb use of intelligence in the Creek War and on the Gulf Coast and reasonably good use of it in the New Orleans campaign. There were occasional lapses, such as when the British got within eight miles of New Orleans before Jackson learned they were near, but he reacted quickly to retrieve the situation by attacking immediately and at night, which set the British back on their heels and gave notice of the unusual sort of man they faced in the campaign.

Jackson is not remembered as much of a writer. His spelling and grammar could suffer, especially when he was in a hurry or angry or under stress. But he wrote a prodigious number of letters, and he was a great believer in using the written word, especially on public occasions, to achieve his ends. He made excellent use of general orders, proclamations, and public addresses on numerous occasions, whether to stir the civilian population in Louisiana or New Orleans, to raise troops in Tennessee or Louisiana, to inspire men before a battle or campaign, or to praise them afterwards. Although increasingly written by his aides—most notably John Reid and Edward Livingston—these documents reflected Jackson's sentiments. They showed how vital he considered public statements to the achievement of his ends.

Jackson also had a good grasp of logistics—how best to move men and material to where they were needed. Like just about every other U.S. commander in the war, he faced recurring shortages of food and other vital supplies, which contractors often could not get to the front in a timely manner. What Jackson had that other commanders lacked was a talent for soldiering on even when there was a failure in the supply service. He might delay a campaign, but he never called it off.

What most set Jackson apart from every other field commander in the war was his determination to overcome obstacles that might have defeated a lesser man. Jackson refused to be slowed by his own suffering, whether from wounds sustained in his duels or brawls in Tennessee or from the recurring bouts of dysentery that afflicted him throughout the war. He did without food or rest when the occasion demanded it, and in the field he never lived better than his men. Jackson expected a lot from himself and expected no less from his men. This meant that he was willing to fire upon those who threatened to go home before he thought their tour of duty was up and that he had no reservations about executing those who were disdainful of discipline or defied orders.

Jackson could act like a ruthless and even paranoid despot when he was defied. It is hard to defend his execution of the six militiamen in February 1815, when the Battle of New Orleans was behind him and the British threat was receding, especially since he pardoned a number of other soldiers who had been condemned to death. It is also hard to justify the tenacity with which Jackson insisted on continuing martial law long after it appeared to be justified. As a practicable matter, the proclamation of martial law in December made good sense (even if not ultimately sustained by the courts), but it hardly needed to be continued after news of the peace treaty arrived in February. Even Jackson conceded that this news was probably true and that it was very likely that the United States would ratify the treaty, thus bringing the war to an end. However, it seems probable that Jackson's ruthless stubbornness to maintain discipline had a lot to do with his ability to get the most out of his men in battle.

The flip side of Jackson's ruthless discipline was his determination to take care of his men. His unwillingness to abandon his men at Natchez early in the war, his willingness to let men sicker than he use his horses, and his readiness to share whatever rations were available with the rank and file spoke volumes about how much he cared about the welfare of his men. There is no evidence that Jackson ever thought that his rank entitled him to any comforts or special privileges that were denied to his men.

Jackson had another indispensable requirement of a successful field commander: He never panicked but instead showed remarkable composure under fire. He saved the day at Enotachopco Creek after his rearguard caved in when he rallied his men and restored order. He also inspired his men in the Night Attack to save two fieldpieces when they were nearly captured. On both occasions Jackson was undoubtedly lucky that he was not killed. He was also lucky in the main battle at New Orleans that Thornton fell behind schedule and could not support the attack against Jackson's main line. But luck always plays a role on the battlefield. Good commanders find a way to profit from it and, conversely, to minimize the impact of bad luck. Jackson certainly fits this mold. He had all the qualities of a top-notch field commander, and this meant that he was never defeated by bad luck and invariably profited from good luck.

Jackson never had the luxury of commanding a force that consisted mainly of experienced regulars or of campaigning in a region developed enough to supply the provisions and equipment that he needed. Most of his men were militia or volunteers or Indians, and their deep-seated commitment to rugged individualism made them difficult to manage. Moreover, in the Creek War and even at New Orleans, Jackson had to contend with long and uncertain supply lines. No other field commander who faced these challenges enjoyed his success. Given the materials that he had to work with and the obstacles he faced, Jackson's success in the field marks him as the preeminent military leader of the War of 1812.

epilogue

An Enduring Legacy

NEWS OF Jackson's victory at New Orleans struck the nation's capital like a thunderbolt on February 4, exactly four weeks after the battle. The Washington *National Intelligencer* considered the matter so important that it put out a special issue to publicize it. Under a headline that read "Glorious Victory! FROM NEW-ORLEANS," the paper reported: "The Enemy, attacking our entrenched Army on the 8th, [was] beaten and repulsed by Jackson and his brave associates, with great slaughter."[1] In response to the news, Washington erupted with joy. From the capital city the news raced up and down the coast, touching off celebrations. Cities were illuminated, parades were held, and there were countless toasts, huzzas, and handshakes. Everywhere news of Jackson's victory gave a huge boost to public morale and national pride.

Ten days later news arrived in Washington that a peace treaty had been signed in Ghent and that the British had already ratified it. Because of bad weather in the Chesapeake, the truce ship bringing the U.S. copy of the treaty and the British instrument of ratification headed instead for New York City, docking there on February 11. The treaty was raced to the nation's capital, and since it called for no U.S. concessions but simply restored the *status quo ante bellum* (the state that had existed before the war), it was approved unanimously by the U.S. Senate on February 16. Later that day the president added his signature in the Octagon House, which had become the temporary executive mansion after the White House was burned.

Madison's signature completed the ratification process. Since the British had already ratified, this ended the war. Both sides sent expresses to all commanders with the news. The next day, Anthony St. John Baker, the British official who brought the Crown's ratification on the truce ship, exchanged ratifications with acting Secretary of State James Monroe, and with this the entire treaty went into effect.

The Resumption of Normal Relations

At the time no one thought this would be the last Anglo-American war. After all, the Treaty of Ghent had settled none of the maritime issues that were in dispute. In fact, those issues were not even mentioned in the agreement. John Quincy Adams, the head of the U.S. peace delegation, thought that the treaty was more of "an unlimited armistice than a peace" because it "left open . . . all the controversies which had produced the war."[2]

Although most Americans shared Adams's view, no one expected a renewal of hostilities any time soon. Both nations were war-weary, both had earned a measure of respect on the battlefield, and neither was likely to forget the challenges of waging offensive war in the North American wilderness. These challenges explain why the United States was unable to make much headway when it was on the offensive in 1812–13 and why the British had no greater success when they were in control in 1814–15. It also explains why the three biggest offensives of the war—against Montreal in 1813, against Plattsburgh in 1814, and against New Orleans in 1815—all failed.

People on both sides were eager to resume normal relations. The Atlantic Ocean was soon filled with merchant vessels flying British and American colors moving British manufactured goods to the United States and American raw materials and commodities to British ports around the world. On the Detroit frontier, a grand pacification ball was held to celebrate the end of the war. Along the Niagara River, where death and destruction had been the greatest, people were also quick to resume their normal commercial and social relations. Farther east, across the long and extended border that stretched from New York to Maine, trade with Canada had never ceased during the war, but now it was legal, and it mushroomed.

The story was much the same on the Gulf Coast, where a sizeable British army was now marking time on Dauphin Island just off Mobile Bay. Food was in short supply, and Britain's nearest possessions, the sugar islands in the West Indies, were nearly two weeks away. Shortly after peace was announced, a U.S. Navy officer who ferried dispatches from Jackson to the British camp on Dauphin Island reported, "They have about 8000 men there, who are almost in a state of starvation. We are now supplying them with provisions of every kind."[3]

New Orleans and the Peace Treaty

The juxtaposition of the news of Jackson's victory and the treaty of peace was not lost on the American people. In the ensuing years, memories faded, and many Americans came to believe that the former had produced the latter, that Jackson's victory had produced a favorable peace settlement. In truth, the Gulf Coast campaign played no role in the peace negotiations. It was not even on the radar of British officials when they considered their options. In fact, the British prime minister, Lord Liverpool, dismissed New Orleans as "one of the most unhealthy [places] in any part of America."[4] The United States was lucky to escape from the war without surrendering any right or territory, although this was lost on the American people. By 1816, *Niles' Register* was claiming that "we did virtually dictate the treaty of Ghent."[5]

That the Battle of New Orleans produced a favorable peace settlement for the United States was only one of a legion of myths that grew up around the battle. Most persistent were the myths that the Kentucky rifle had won the battle (it was mainly artillery); that Jean Lafitte and his pirates had played a central role (an exaggeration based on a combination of the romantic appeal of pirates and a fake Lafitte diary that surfaced in the 1950s); that the British planned to sack the city if they won—known as the "beauty and booty" myth—(there was no credible evidence for this notion); and that the British would not have surrendered southern Louisiana if they had prevailed (again, no evidence). These myths persisted because they endowed the victory with greater meaning, fostered an appealing self-image, and promoted a notion of unconventional Yankee success that Americans found attractive.

Once the notion had faded that the Battle of New Orleans had produced a favorable peace settlement, it was replaced by another myth, that the battle was fought after the war was over. But this notion is also untrue. Had this been a typical European war, the signing of the Treaty of Ghent on December 24, 1814, might have ended the contest, but the British, having been burned when the United States demanded changes before ratifying earlier agreements, insisted on a clause in the Ghent treaty that provided for ending the war only after both nations had ratified. Although the British ratified on December 27, getting the treaty across the Atlantic delayed the U.S. ratification until February 16, 1815, which was five weeks after the Battle of New Orleans.

There were also many lesser myths that showed up in the mountain of sketches, drawings, paintings, and other works of art produced in later years to celebrate Jackson's victory. The most common were that the two armies were near enough to engage in close combat (not so); that soldiers on both sides had a clear field of fire (there was too little light and too much smoke); that Jackson's line was constructed of cotton bales (they were earlier tried as supports for the gun platforms but were removed because they were too flammable); that the Scottish 93rd Regiment of Foot wore kilts (they actually wore tartan trousers); or that Jackson was a visible target (even on horseback he was difficult to see behind the American line).

The Significance of 1812

This is not to suggest that the Battle of New Orleans was unimportant or that the War of 1812 had no impact on the postwar world. Far from it. The war may have been a small and inconclusive contest, but it was fraught with a host of consequences that are little appreciated today. It boosted American self-confidence, earned respect abroad, and with the decisive victories over the Indians in both the Northwest and Southwest promoted territorial expansion. The Indians were, in fact, the biggest losers in the war. For them this was in many ways their last hurrah, their last opportunity to ally with a foreign power and shape the destiny of the continent.

The war also led to the birth of the modern American military establishment because after 1815 most Democratic-Republicans embraced the need for military preparedness in time of peace. The U.S. Navy, which had earned its laurels in the single-ship duels on the high seas, benefited the most from this development. Both the army and the navy emerged from the war with a commitment to professionalism, and the heroes of 1812 dominated both services until the Civil War.

The Battle of New Orleans as portrayed not long after 1815. American popular imagination has always placed American riflemen behind bales of cotton. In fact, they fought behind earthworks, and artillery caused most of the British casualties. The painting rightly demonstrates the well-covered position of the defenders and the varied makeup of Jackson's force. (The Granger Collection, New York)

Much the same happened in the political arena. No fewer than seven future presidents either launched or boosted their public careers during this war: James Monroe (who served in Madison's wartime cabinet); John Quincy Adams (who helped forge the Treaty of Ghent); Andrew Jackson (the hero of the Creek War and New Orleans); Martin Van Buren (who served in the New York senate); William Henry Harrison (the hero of Tippecanoe and the Thames); John Tyler (a strong supporter of the war who organized a volunteer militia unit to defend Richmond); and Zachary Taylor (who as a captain in the U.S. Army oversaw the defense of Fort Harrison in the Indiana Territory in 1812). Countless other veterans of the war managed to parlay their service into public office afterwards. The Battle of the Thames alone produced one president (Harrison), one vice president (Richard M. Johnson), three governors, three lieutenant governors, four U.S. senators, and 20 congressmen.

The war also helped forge an American identity. Sayings such as "Don't give up the ship" and "We have met the enemy and they are ours" entered the public lexicon and are still used today. Americans also embraced a host of symbols from the war. Among the most enduring were "Old Ironsides" (which is still a commissioned ship in the U.S. Navy), the Fort McHenry flag (which is on display at the Smithsonian), Uncle Sam (a nickname that came into general usage during the war), "The Star-Spangled Banner" (which became the national anthem in 1931), and the Kentucky rifle (which was actually the Pennsylvania rifle and played only a modest role in the war). These symbols loomed large in the nation's culture after the war and helped citizens in the fledgling republic better understand who they were and what it meant to be an American.

Jackson and New Orleans

The two biggest symbols in the immediate postwar world—Jackson and New Orleans—played a special role in boosting American pride and forging the national identity. Jackson emerged as the biggest winner. In his address in the public service of thanksgiving after the Battle of New Orleans, Abbé Guillaume Dubourg suggested that Jackson was an instrument of God. This claim was widely repeated in the postwar years because it nicely dovetailed with two other commonly held notions: (1) that Americans were the chosen people of God who enjoyed special protection from Providence; and (2) that in time of crisis a leader would spring up from the people to lead citizen soldiers to victory over the republic's enemies.

But if Providence had chosen to protect Americans through the agency of Jackson, it was because Jackson was the only man who could defeat the British at New Orleans. It was widely believed at the time—and likely would be supported by many historians today—that of all the American military commanders only Jackson had that rare combination of talent and will to carry his motley army to victory. If contemporaries saw Jackson as the indispensable man at New Orleans, they also considered him on a par with the incomparable Washington, although as a man of the people closely identified with the West, he was a better fit for the postwar era.

That Jackson was not a professional military man but an untutored militia officer added to his appeal. In later years, he was often described as a natural, instinctive, or intuitive genius. That American militia, called from their peacetime pursuits, had defeated an accomplished veteran army made the story more compelling. Adding still more to the national myth was the no-

After the victory at New Orleans and word of the Peace Treaty of Ghent, Americans indulged in an orgy of patriotism and self-congratulation. Citizen soldiers had defeated the veterans of European wars at Fort McHenry and New Orleans, and the future of the young republic looked bright. The popularity of "The Star-Spangled Banner" spread rapidly across the country. Prints, banners, pottery, china, and all manner of household decoration celebrated Jackson and the glorious victory at New Orleans. This wall hanging immortalized Jackson and his men and, for good measure, portrayed other—mostly naval—victories on the edges. ("The Glorious Victory of New Orleans," engraving on cloth. Historic New Orleans Collection, Acc. No. 1947.19)

tion that it was not only farmers from the borderlands who had done the job, but that their chosen instrument had been the long rifle, and that they had succeeded because they were crack shots.

Jackson himself propagated this myth two weeks after the battle in an address thanking his troops. He spoke of how the British had been "cut down by the untutored courage of American militia" with "a fire incessantly kept up, directed with calmness and with unerring aim."[6] George M. Troup of Georgia made a similar point in the halls of Congress: "The farmers of the country," he said, were "triumphantly victorious over the conquerors of the conquerors of Europe. 'I came, I saw, I conquered,' says the American husbandman, fresh from his plow."[7]

Remembered this way, the Battle of New Orleans, coupled with William Henry Harrison's victory over an Anglo-Indian force at the Thames in 1813, gave new life to the militia myth, that is, the idea that citizen soldiers offer the best means of defending the republic in time of crisis. This myth was born at Lexington and Concord and Bunker Hill in 1775 and reinforced by the successful partisan warfare that followed in the American Revolution. Although regulars did most of the significant fighting in both wars with Britain, Americans took comfort in remembering their history otherwise. The militia myth was a powerful and enduring myth, and it coexisted uneasily with the modern military establishment that was also forged by the War of 1812.

To the modern eye, Jackson looks like a bundle of contradictions with a penchant for arbitrary if not despotic rule. Although an enemy of privilege and a spokesman for democracy, he was a leading member of Tennessee's landed gentry. Although an Indian-hater who eagerly seized an opportunity to kill off Native Americans and confiscate their lands, he adopted an Indian boy and groomed him for the U.S. Military Academy. He was a slave trader and slave owner, but he welcomed free blacks into his army. He loved his troops and looked after their welfare, but he was far less indulgent to militia and volunteers than any other U.S. commander in the war. He lectured his superiors on policy matters and ignored their orders when it suited him but did not always welcome unsolicited suggestions from his own subordinates; in fact, he insisted on unthinking obedience to his orders. He had an explosive temper that often led to violence, but he rarely raised his voice to his wife or friends.

Jackson's enemies knew his weaknesses, and they sought to portray him as a violent anti-republican dictator who menaced basic rights. In the election of 1828 they even circulated a notorious series of flyers, known as the "Coffin Handbills," that showed pictures of coffins to remind the public of the citizen soldiers Jackson had executed during the War of 1812. The handbills were so shocking they may have backfired; they were not resurrected when Jackson ran for reelection in 1832. Most Americans preferred to focus on those Jacksonian traits that they considered central to the national identity: courage and individualism, patriotism and devotion to party, and a sense of duty and loyalty. Moreover, with his paradoxical belief in democracy and slavery as well as his commitment to Indian removal and territorial expansion, Jackson seemed to embody the central themes of postwar America. In fact, so aptly did he symbolize the era that even today scholars call it the Age of Jackson.

Even though the Battle of New Orleans made Jackson a great national hero, his future did not lie with the military. He remained in the U.S. Army as one of its two principal officers until 1821, but his penchant for lecturing his superiors and ignoring or defying their orders only got worse. He caused a public sensation in 1818 when he exceeded orders by invading Spanish Florida, where he executed two British subjects for stirring up the Seminoles. But his independent command style was increasingly out of tune with a postwar army that was becoming ever more professional, nonpartisan, and mindful of civilian authority. Rather, Jackson's future lay in the political arena, where he was twice elected president and became the dominant figure in that office between Jefferson and Lincoln.

The Battle of New Orleans was no less influential in shaping the postwar age. Although it had no impact on the peace treaty or the outcome of the war, it had a profound and lasting effect on shaping how Americans remembered the war. As the Boston *Patriot* put it, "The brilliant and unparalleled victory at *New-Orleans* has closed the war in a blaze of Glory and placed America on the very pinnacle of fame."[8] Jackson's great victory trumped even the peace treaty. "The terms of the treaty are yet unknown to us," boasted Congressman Charles J. Ingersoll in early 1815. "But the victory at Orleans has rendered them glorious and honorable, be they what they may. . . . Who is not proud to feel himself an American—our wrongs revenged—our rights recognized!"[9]

Much of the history of the war quickly faded from public memory. Americans forgot the causes of the war, the military defeats, the economic depression, the Treasury's insolvency, and the financial chaos. They forgot how close the fragile republic had come to military defeat, national bankruptcy, and political disruption if not disunion. Instead, every year on January 8, Americans celebrated Jackson's great victory much as they celebrated Independence Day on July 4.

Jackson's victory transformed the entire war into a glorious U.S. triumph, a triumph in which the young republic had beat back a British attempt to

"Genl. Andrew Jackson, 1828. Protector & defender
of beauty and booty, Orleans." Jackson as he appeared
in a tract supporting his candidacy for president in
1828. As the hero of New Orleans, he stood for the
protection of womanly honor and the rights of property, although there is little evidence that the British
planned to sack the city. For many Americans after
1815, especially in the western states, Jackson epito-
mized important frontier virtues: He was close to
nature, tough in the face of challenges, and enjoyed
good luck that seemed to reflect divine destiny. One
could argue, as did John William Ward long after
Jackson's death, that Americans liked Jackson because they wanted to think of themselves in the same
way. (Engraving by C. G. Childs based on a painting
by Joseph Wood, Library of Congress)

seize American territory and restore colonial rule, a triumph in which western farmers carrying long rifles had saved the young republic by decisively
defeating a powerful and imperious foe. As Jackson succinctly put it, at New
Orleans "the invincibles of Wellington were foiled, the Conquerors of Europe Conquered."[10]

The public memory of New Orleans increased the impact of just about every other positive memory of the war. It made the other victories sweeter, and it boosted the reputation of anyone, whether in civil or military life, who had done something to make those victories possible. It also gave greater meaning to the sayings and symbols that came out of the war. The Battle of New Orleans, in short, transformed the entire war, at least in the eyes of Americans, into a glorious triumph and a great benchmark in the march of U.S. progress and in the broader history of mankind.

A Lasting Peace

Jackson's victory at New Orleans had another effect: It contributed to a lasting peace. The British public quickly forgot the battle and even the war, but the British government did not have the luxury of doing so, at least not as long as it was responsible for protecting Canada from the growing colossus to the south. It did not take British officials long to conclude that cultivating native allies and pumping money into beefing up Canada's defenses were unlikely to do the job. Instead, the British jettisoned their native allies and adopted a policy of accommodating the United States, even though this meant occasionally sacrificing imperial interests elsewhere (even in Canada).

Anglo-American relations remained rocky in the decades after 1815, and there was even an occasional war scare, but in time the British policy of accommodation paid off. Most of the maritime issues that had once generated so much heat faded away, and other differences were resolved peacefully by treaty. By the end of the nineteenth century a relationship that had once been so contentious and antagonistic had turned into a genuine accord.

Although a few of the maritime issues surfaced again when World War I erupted in 1914, by then war between Great Britain and the United States had become unlikely, if not unthinkable, because the two English-speaking nations had so much in common. This included not only growing trade— which increased twenty-fold between 1815 and 1914—but also a common language and similar culture as well as a commitment to democracy, the rule of law, and free markets. Little wonder that when the United States entered the First World War in 1917, it was as a co-belligerent of Britain. By World War II the Anglo-American accord had blossomed into a full-fledged alliance, one that has persisted down to the present day. That enduring alliance is yet another legacy of the War of 1812.

Notes

Prologue: America at a Crossroads

1. G. C. Moore Smith, ed., *The Autobiography of Lieutenant-General Sir Harry Smith*, 2 vols. (London, 1901), 1:247.
2. Gene A. Smith, ed., *A British Eyewitness at the Battle of New Orleans: The Memoir of Royal Navy Admiral Robert Aitchison, 1808–1827* (New Orleans, 2004), 62.

CHAPTER ONE: Completing the Revolution

1. Winfield Scott, *Memoirs of Lieut.-General Scott*, 2 vols. (New York, 1864), 1:31; Porter to secretary of war, July 27, 1813, in U.S. Department of War, *Letters Received by the Secretary of War, Unregistered Series, 1789–1861*, Microfilm Series M222, National Archives, Washington, DC, reel 9.
2. Speech of George M. Troup, April 30, 1812, in U.S. Congress, *Annals of Congress: Debates and Proceedings in the Congress of the United States, 1789–1824*, 42 vols. (Washington, DC, 1834–56), Twelfth Congress, 1st session, 1359 (hereafter cited as *AC*, 12-1, and similarly for other sessions).
3. Quoted in William A. Burrell to Wilson Cary Nicholas, May 23, 1812, in Nicholas Papers, University of Virginia, Charlottesville, VA.
4. Monroe to John Taylor, June 13, 1812, in Monroe Papers, Library of Congress, Washington, DC, microfilm edition, reel 5.
5. Charles Cutts to William Plumer, December 11, 1811, in Plumer Papers, Library of Congress, Washington, DC, microfilm edition, reel 3.
6. Daniel D. Tompkins to Robert Macomb, July 12, 1812, in Hugh Hastings, ed., *Public Papers of Daniel D. Tompkins, Governor of New York, 1807–1817*, 3 vols. (New York and Albany, 1898–1902), 3:26–27.
7. Jefferson to William Duane, August 4, 1812, in Jefferson Papers, Library of Congress, Washington, DC, microfilm edition, reel 46.
8. Speech of John Randolph, December 10, 1811, in *AC*, 12-1, 447.
9. Jacob Brown to secretary of war, November 28, 1814, in Brown Papers, Library of Congress, Washington, DC.
10. Statement of American officers, February 20, 1813, in John Brannan, ed., *Official Letters of the Military and Naval Officers of the United States, during the War with Great Britain in the Years 1812, 13, 14, & 15* (Washington, DC, 1823), 135.

11. Charles J. Ingersoll, *Historical Sketch of the Second War between the United States of America, and Great Britain*, 2 vols. (Philadelphia, 1845–49), 1:102.

12. Philadelphia *Aurora*, October 29, 1812.

13. Secretary of the navy to Isaac Chauncey, January 27, 1813, in U.S. Department of the Navy, *Letters Sent by the Secretary of the Navy to Officers, 1798–1868*, Microfilm Series M149, National Archives, Washington, DC, reel 10.

14. Perry to Harrison, September 10, 1813, in Benson J. Lossing, *The Pictorial Field-Book of the War of 1812* (New York, 1868), 530. Perry actually took two ships, two schooners, one brig, and a sloop.

15. Quoted in Thomas D. Clark, "Kentucky in the Northwest Campaign," in Philip P. Mason, ed., *After Tippecanoe: Some Aspects of the War of 1812* (East Lansing, MI, 1963), 94.

16. Daniel D. Tompkins to secretary of war, January 2, 1814, in Hastings, *Papers of Daniel D. Tompkins*, 3:408.

17. London *Times*, May 24, 1814.

18. Campbell to John Walbach, May 18, 1814, in U.S. Department of War, *Confidential and Unofficial Letters Sent by the Secretary of War, Registered Series, 1801–1870*, Microfilm Series M221, National Archives, Washington, DC, reel 51 (hereafter cited as WD [M221]).

19. Proclamation of Alexander Cochrane, April 2, 1814, in William S. Dudley and Michael J. Crawford, eds., *The Naval War of 1812: A Documentary History*, 4 vols. (Washington, DC, 1985–), 3:60.

20. Cockburn to Alexander Cochrane, July 17, 1814, in Dudley and Crawford, *Naval War*, 3:156; and Cockburn, quoted in Frank A. Cassell, "Slaves of the Chesapeake Bay Area and the War of 1812," *Journal of Negro History* 57 (April 1972), 151.

21. Lexington *Reporter*, August 7, 1813.

22. Sir George Prevost to John W. Croker, August 27, 1814, in Ernest A. Cruikshank, ed., *The Documentary History of the Campaign on the Niagara Frontier*, 9 vols. (Welland, ON, [1896]–1908), 1:180.

23. Secretary of the navy to James Madison, [October 15, 1814], in Madison Papers, Library of Congress, Washington, DC, microfilm edition, reel 16.

24. Andrei Dashkov to Nikolai Rumiantsev, January 1, 1815, in Nina K. Bashkina et al., eds., *The United States and Russia: The Beginning of Relations, 1765–1815* [Washington, DC, 1980], 1100.

CHAPTER TWO: The Making of a Hero

1. Jackson to Amos Kendall, January 9, 1844, in Sam B. Smith et al., eds., *The Papers of Andrew Jackson*, 9 vols. to date (Knoxville, TN, 1980–), 1:9n4.

2. Jackson to Rachel Jackson, August 5, 1814, in Smith, *Papers of Andrew Jackson*, 3:105.

3. Jackson to James Robertson, January 11, 1798, in Smith, *Papers of Andrew Jackson*, 1:165.

4. Quoted in James Parton, *Life of Andrew Jackson*, 3 vols. (New York, 1859–60), 1:104.

5. Quoted in Parton, *Life of Andrew Jackson*, 1:249.

6. Parton, *Life of Andrew Jackson*, 1:154.

7. Andrew Jackson, "Stop the Runaway," Nashville *Tennessee Gazette*, October 3, 1804, in Smith, *Papers of Andrew Jackson*, 2:41.

8. Jackson to John Overton, January 22, 1798, in Smith, *Papers of Andrew Jackson*, 1:170.

9. Jackson to Harrison, November 28, 1811, in Smith, *Papers of Andrew Jackson*, 2:270.

10. Jackson to Willie Blount, June 5, 1812, in Smith, *Papers of Andrew Jackson*, 2:301.

11. Jackson to Daniel Smith, February 11, 1807, in Smith, *Papers of Andrew Jackson*, 2:155.

12. Jackson to Dearborn, March 17, 1807, in Smith, *Papers of Andrew Jackson*, 2:156.

13. Jackson to William Cocke, June 25, 1798, in Smith, *Papers of Andrew Jackson*, 1:204; Jackson to John Sevier, May 10, 1797, in A. V. Goodpasture, "Genesis of the Jackson-Sevier Feud," *American Historical Magazine* 5 (April 1900), 120.

14. Jackson to Avery, August 12, 1788, in Smith, *Papers of Andrew Jackson*, 1:12.

15. Jackson to the Public, [October 10, 1803], in Smith, *Papers of Andrew Jackson*, 1:379.

16. Benton to the Public, September 10, 1813, in Smith, *Papers of Andrew Jackson*, 2:425.

17. Parton, *Life of Andrew Jackson*, 1:305.

18. Jefferson, quoted in Parton, *Life of Andrew Jackson*, 1:219.

CHAPTER THREE: The Creek War

1. Jackson to the 2nd Division, March 7, 1812, in Smith, *Papers of Andrew Jackson*, 2:291.

2. Jackson to Rachel Jackson, February 22, 1813, in Smith, *Papers of Andrew Jackson*, 2:370.

3. Jackson to George Washington Campbell, [November 29, 1812], in Smith, *Papers of Andrew Jackson*, 2:344.

4. Quoted in Parton, *Life of Andrew Jackson*, 1:375.

5. Jackson to [Felix Grundy], March 15, 1813, in Smith, *Papers of Andrew Jackson*, 2:386.

6. Nashville *Whig*, quoted in Robert V. Remini, *Andrew Jackson*, 3 vols. (Baltimore and New York, 1977–84), 1:180.

7. Duke de la Rochefoucauld Liancourt, *Travels through the United States of North America, the Country of the Iroquois, and Upper Canada, in the Years 1795, 1796, and 1797,* 4 vols., 2nd ed. (London, 1800), 2:466.

8. Jefferson to David Bailie Warden, December 29, 1813, in J. Jefferson Looney et al., eds., *The Papers of Thomas Jefferson: Retirement Series*, 7 vols. to date (Princeton, NJ, 2004–), 7:91.

9. *Niles' Register* 5 (September 13, 1813), 43.

10. Jackson to Willie Blount, June 4 and July 3, 1812, in Smith, *Papers of Andrew Jackson*, 2:300 and 307–8; Sevier, quoted in Tom Kanon, "The Kidnapping of Martha Crawley and Settler-Indian Relations Prior to the War of 1812," *Tennessee Historical Quarterly* 64 (Spring 2005), 7.

11. Quoted in John F. H. Claiborne, *Life and Times of Gen. Sam. Dale, The Mississippi Partisan* (New York, 1860), 128–29.

12. William Claiborne, quoted in H. S. Halbert and T. H. Ball, *The Creek War of 1813 and 1814* (Chicago, 1895), 299.

13. Harry Toulmin to Raleigh *Register*, September 7, 1813, reprinted in *Niles' Register* 5 (October 16, 1813), 105.

14. Parton, *Life of Andrew Jackson*, 1:428.

15. General Orders of November 7, 1813, in Andrew Jackson Papers, Library of Congress, Washington, DC, microfilm edition, reel 61.

16. Quoted in John Reid and John Henry Eaton, *The Life of Andrew Jackson*, ed. Frank Lawrence Owsley, Jr. (1817; reprinted, University, AL, 1974), 42–43.

17. Coffee to Andrew Jackson, November 4, 1813, in Brannan, *Official Letters*, 256.

18. David Crockett, *A Narrative of the Life of David Crockett, of the State of Tennessee* (Philadelphia, 1834), 43–44.

19. Jackson to Rachel Jackson, November 12, 1813, in Smith, *Papers of Andrew Jackson*, 2:449.

20. Quoted in Parton, *Life of Andrew Jackson*, 1:432.

21. Jackson to John Armstrong, December 16, 1813, in Smith, *Papers of Andrew Jackson*, 2:493.

22. Coffee to Captain Donelson, December 22, 1813, in Parton, *Life of Andrew Jackson*, 1:478.

23. Parton, *Life of Andrew Jackson*, 1:463.

24. Jackson to Willie Blount, [December, 1813], in Parton, *Life of Andrew Jackson*, 1:481.

25. Jackson to Rachel Jackson, December 29, 1813, and Jackson to Robert Hays, January 4, 1814, in Smith, *Papers of Andrew Jackson*, 2:515–16, and 3:6.

26. Reid and Eaton, *Life of Andrew Jackson*, 136.

27. Crockett, *Narrative of the Life of David Crockett*, 50.

28. Jackson to Rachel Jackson, January 28, 1814, in Smith, *Papers of Andrew Jackson*, 3:20.

29. Jackson to William Lewis, February 21, 1814, in Jackson Papers, Supplement, microfilm edition, Scholarly Resources, Wilmington, DE, reel 3.

30. Jackson to William Carroll, February 17, 1814, in Smith, *Papers of Andrew Jackson*, 3:31.

31. Parton, *Life of Andrew Jackson*, 1:508.

32. General Order, John Wood, March 14, 1814, in Smith, *Papers of Andrew Jackson*, 3:49.

33. Reid and Eaton, *Life of Andrew Jackson*, 143.

34. Jackson to Rachel Jackson, April 1, 1814, in Smith, *Papers of Andrew Jackson*, 3:54.

35. Address of Andrew Jackson, April 2, 1814, in Smith, *Papers of Andrew Jackson*, 3:58.

36. Quoted in letter of Anne Royall, December 15, 1817, in Lucille Griffith, ed., *Letters from Alabama, 1817–1822, by Anne Royall* (University, AL, 1969), 91–92.

37. Jesse Wharton to Andrew Jackson, February 16, 1815, in Smith, *Papers of Andrew Jackson*, 3:280.

38. Pinckney, quoted in Parton, *Life of Andrew Jackson*, 1:498.

39. Thomas Bibb to Andrew Jackson, November 10, 1814, in Smith, *Papers of Andrew Jackson*, 3:184.

CHAPTER FOUR: The British on the Gulf Coast

1. Rachel Jackson to Eliza Kingsley, April 27, 1821, in Parton, *Life of Andrew Jackson*, 2:595.

2. Lord Bathurst to Ross, September 6, 1814, in Admiralty Records 1/4360, pp. 58–65 (transcript supplied by Naval History and Heritage Command, Washington, DC).

3. Vincent Gray, quoted in Frank L. Owsley, Jr., *Struggle for the Gulf Borderlands: The Creek War and the Battle of New Orleans, 1812–1815* (Tuscaloosa, AL, 1981), 121.

4. Jackson to secretary of war, July 30, 1814, in WD (M221), reel 63.

5. Jackson to Mateo Gonzalez Manrique, August 24, 1814, in Smith, *Papers of Andrew Jackson*, 3:119.

6. Jackson to John Coffee, October 20, 1814, in Smith, *Papers of Andrew Jackson*, 3:169.

7. Jackson to James Monroe, October 26, 1814, in Smith, *Papers of Andrew Jackson*, 3:173.

8. Jackson to James Monroe, November 20, 1814, in Smith, *Papers of Andrew Jackson*, 3:192.

9. Proclamation of Edward Nicolls, August 29, 1814, in *Niles' Register* 7 (November 5, 1814), 134–35.

10. Proclamation of Andrew Jackson, September 21, 1814, in Arsène Lacarrière Latour, *Historical Memoir of the War in West Florida and Louisiana in 1814–15* (1816; edited and expanded by Gene A. Smith, Gainesville, FL, 1999), 204–5.

11. Proclamation of Andrew Jackson, September 21, 1814, in Latour, *Historical Memoir*, 206.

12. [John Windship] to William Plumer, March 20, 1814, in Plumer Papers, New Hampshire Historical Society, Concord, NH, microfilm edition, reel 2.

13. Thomas Flournoy to secretary of war, March 14, 1814, in WD (M221), reel 52.

14. Letter from New Orleans, September 9, 1814, in Washington *National Intelligencer,* October 3, 1814.

15. Latour, *Historical Memoir,* 59; Francois-Xavier Martin, *The History of Louisiana, From the Earliest Period,* 2 vols. (New Orleans, 1827–29), 2:340.

16. Latour, *Historical Memoir,* 59.

CHAPTER FIVE: A Glorious Victory

1. Jackson to the Citizens of New Orleans, December 15, 1814, in Smith, *Papers of Andrew Jackson,* 3:204–5.

2. Proclamation of Andrew Jackson, September 21, 1814, in Latour, *Historical Memoir,* 204.

3. Edward Codrington to wife, December 23 and 27, 1814, in Jane Bourchier, *Memoir of the Life of Admiral Sir Edward Codrington,* 2 vols. (London, 1873), 1:332–33.

4. [George R. Gleig], *A Subaltern in America, Comprising His Narrative of the Campaigns of the British Army . . . during the Late War* (Philadelphia, 1833), 221.

5. Jackson to Louisiana General Assembly, December 31, 1814, in Smith, *Papers of Andrew Jackson,* 3:226.

6. Robert Rennie, quoted in Alexander Dickson, "Artillery Services in North America in 1814 and 1815," *Journal of the Society for Army Historical Research,* 8 (July 1929), 149.

7. [Gleig], *Subaltern in America,* 250.

8. Smith, *British Eyewitness at the Battle of New Orleans,* 62.

9. Captain John H. Cooke (a veteran of the Napoleonic Wars), quoted in Parton, *Life of Andrew Jackson,* 2:184.

10. Quoted in Wilbur S. Brown, *The Amphibious Campaign for West Florida and Louisiana, 1814–1815: A Critical Review of Strategy and Tactics at New Orleans* (University, AL, 1969), 139.

11. Dickson, "Artillery Services in North America," 161.

12. Moore Smith, *Autobiography of Harry Smith,* 1:247.

13. "A Contemporary Account of the Battle of New Orleans by a Soldier in the Ranks," *Louisiana Historical Quarterly* 9 (January 1926), 11.

14. Letter from New Orleans, January 13, 1815, in *Niles' Register* 7 (February 11, 1815), 379.

15. Ibid., 378.

16. "A Contemporary Account of the Battle of New Orleans," 14.

17. George R. Gleig, *Campaigns of the British Army at Washington and New Orleans, 1814–1815,* new ed. (London, 1879), 182.

18. Quoted in *Niles' Register* 8 (March–September, 1815, Supplement), 184.

19. Moore Smith, *Autobiography of Harry Smith,* 1:241.

20. Washington *National Intelligencer,* February 7, 1815.

21. Proceedings of a Court of Inquiry relative to the Retreat on the Right Bank of the Mississippi, on the 8th of January, 1815, in Latour, *Historical Memoir,* 299.

22. Jackson to Claiborne, February 5, 1815, in Smith, *Papers of Andrew Jackson*, 3:270.

23. Jackson to Robert Hays, February 4, 1815, in Smith, *Papers of Andrew Jackson*, 3:269.

24. Jackson to Philip Pipkin, September 12, 1814, in Smith, *Papers of Andrew Jackson*, 3:136.

25. Jackson to David Holmes, January 18, 1815, in Smith, *Papers of Andrew Jackson*, 3:249.

26. Jackson to secretary of war, January 19, 1815, in Latour, *Historical Memoir*, 241.

27. Jackson to secretary of war, [ca. April 27, 1815], in Smith, *Papers of Andrew Jackson*, 3:350.

28. Louis Louaillier to New Orleans *Courier de la Louisiana*, March 3, 1815, in Martin, *History of Louisiana*, 2:389, 392.

29. Report of Court, [March 21, 1815], in Jackson Papers, Library of Congress, reel 17.

30. Jackson to the Citizens and Soldiers of New Orleans, [March 31, 1815], in Smith, *Papers of Andrew Jackson*, 3:337.

31. Jackson to unknown, [ca. March 31, 1815], in Smith, *Papers of Andrew Jackson*, 3:337–38.

32. Ibid., 3:338.

33. *Ex parte Milligan* (1866), in Stephen K. Williams, ed., *Cases Argued and Decided in the Supreme Court of the United States*, Book 18, Law ed. (Rochester, NY), 298.

Epilogue: An Enduring Legacy

1. Washington *National Intelligencer*, reprinted in Bedford (PA) *True American*, February 9, 1915.

2. John Quincy Adams to Louisa Catherine Adams, January 3, 1815, in Worthington C. Ford, ed., *Writings of John Quincy Adams*, 7 vols. (New York, 1913–17), 5:261.

3. Letter from an officer in New Orleans to his friend in Charleston, March 24, 1815, printed in Washington *National Intelligencer*, May 10, 1815.

4. Liverpool to George Canning, December 28, 1814, in Duke of Wellington, [son of Iron Duke], ed., *Supplementary Dispatches, Correspondence, and Memoranda of Field Marshall Arthur, Duke of Wellington, K.G.*, 15 vols. (London, 1858–72), 9:513.

5. *Niles' Register* 11 (September 14, 1816), 40.

6. Jackson to American troops, January 21, 1815, in Latour, *Historical Memoir*, 338.

7. Speech of George M. Troup, February 16, 1815, in *AC*, 13–3, 1156.

8. Boston *Patriot*, reprinted in Concord *New-Hampshire Patriot*, February 21, 1815.

9. Speech of Charles J. Ingersoll, February 16, 1815, in *AC*, 13–3, 1159, 1161.

10. Jackson to Louisiana Militia, March 7, 1815, in Smith, *Papers of Andrew Jackson*, 3:304.

Suggested Further Reading

The literature on the War of 1812, Andrew Jackson, and the Battle of New Orleans is huge. For an overview of the war, see Donald R. Hickey, *The War of 1812: A Forgotten Conflict* (Bicentennial edition, 2012). The best work presenting the British/Canadian side of the story is J. Mackay Hitsman, *The Incredible War of 1812: A Military History* (1965, updated by Donald E. Graves, 1999). For the origins of the war, see Reginald Horsman, *The Causes of the War of 1812* (1969). For Tennessee's role in the war, readers should consult Tom Kanon's fine work, *Tennesseans at War, 1812–1815: Andrew Jackson, The Creek War, and the Battle of New Orleans* (2014).

For Andrew Jackson, the classic biography is James Parton, *Life of Andrew Jackson*, 3 vols. (1859–60). This is such a richly textured study, full of fascinating detail, that it is a pure joy to read. It may well be the best American biography written in the nineteenth century. Parton's judgments are fair and sensible, and except for occasionally relying too heavily on dubious sources, his work is generally sound. Another nineteenth-century work that is less reliable but still useful is Alexander Walker, *Jackson and New Orleans* (1856). This book was also issued under the title *The Life of Andrew Jackson* (1867) with a six-page supplementary chapter on Jackson's postwar career.

The modern equivalent of Parton's work is Robert V. Remini, *Andrew Jackson*, 3 vols. (1977–84). Another comprehensive biography that is still serviceable is John Spencer Bassett, *The Life of Andrew Jackson,* 2 vols. (1911). There are two shorter treatments of Jackson that stand out. Remini produced a one-volume abridgement of his longer work under the title of *Life of Andrew Jackson* (1988), and W. H. Brands published *Andrew Jackson: His Life and Times* (2005).

For those who would like to sample Jackson's own writings, see John S. Bassett, ed., *Correspondence of Andrew Jackson*, 6 vols. (1926–33), which covers Jackson's entire life; and Sam B. Smith et al., eds., *The Papers of Andrew Jackson*, 9 vols. to date (1980–), which so far covers up through 1831.

Creek society and the Creek War have attracted considerable scholarly attention. The best overall treatment of Creek society is Claudio Saunt, *A New Order of Things: Property, Power, and the Transformation of the Creek Indians, 1733–1816* (1999). Also valuable is Kathryn E. Holland Braund, *Deerskins and Duffels: The Creek Indian Trade with Anglo-America, 1785–1815* (2nd edition, 2008). For the Creek War, see Saunt's work above; Frank L. Owsley, Jr., *Struggle for the Gulf Borderlands: The Creek War and the Battle of New Orleans, 1812–1815* (1981); and a book of essays that Braund co-edited with several others, *Tohopeka: Rethinking the Creek War and the War of 1812* (2012). For a fine treatment of one of the opening battles, see Gregory A. Waselkov, *A Conquering Spirit: Fort Mims and the Redstick War of 1813–1814* (2009). For works that focus on Jackson's role in the war, see David S. Heidler and Jeanne T. Heidler, *Old Hickory's War: Andrew Jackson and the Quest for Empire* (1996), and Robert Remini, *Andrew Jackson & His Indian Wars* (2001).

There is no good study of the Gulf Coast in this period, but two studies that focus on American interest in the region stand out: James G. Cusick, *The Other War of 1812: The Patriot War and the American Invasion of Spanish Florida* (2007), and J. C. A. Stagg, *Borderlands in Borderlands: James Madison and the Spanish-American Frontier, 1776–1821* (2009).

For the war on the Gulf Coast the two best American studies are Owsley, cited above, and Wilburt S. Brown, *The Amphibious Campaign for West Florida and Louisiana, 1814–1815: A Critical Review of Strategy and Tactics at New Orleans* (1969). Also excellent is the study by British subject Robin Reilly, *The British at the Gates: The New Orleans Campaign in the War of 1812* (rev. ed., 2002). All three studies are well researched and thoughtful and nicely complement one another. Robert V. Remini has an excellent short study focusing on the main battle, *The Battle of New Orleans: Andrew Jackson and America's First Military Victory* (2001).

For a useful contemporary account that is loaded with illuminating documents, see Arsène Lacarrière Latour, *Historical Memoir of the War in West Florida and Louisiana in 1814–15* (1816, edited and expanded by Gene A. Smith, 1999). For a study that examines Jackson's declaration of martial law and traces the way it was viewed up through the Civil War, see Matthew Warshauer, *Andrew Jackson and the Politics of Martial Law: Nationalism, Civil Liberties, and Partisanship* (2006).

For postwar America, three classic studies from more than a half century ago are a good place to start: George Dangerfield, *The Era of Good Feelings* (1952); John William Ward, *Andrew Jackson: Symbol for an Age* (1955); and Arthur M. Schlesinger, Jr., *The Age of Jackson* (1945). For a short modern topical introduction to the period, see Daniel Feller, *The Jacksonian Promise: America, 1815–1840* (2005). For longer modern treatments, see Sean Wilentz, *The Rise of American Democracy: Jefferson to Lincoln* (2005), and Daniel Walker Howe, *What Hath God Wrought: The Transformation of America, 1815–1848* (2007). The bibliographical essay in Feller, the notes in Wilentz, and the notes and bibliography in Howe will guide the reader to a host of other modern works.

There is no comprehensive study of the legacy of the War of 1812. Until we get one, interested readers can find an introduction to the subject in the Conclusion of Hickey's work cited above.

Index

Note: Battle sites and other place names are followed in parentheses by the modern state, province, or country in which they are located